Instructor Review Access

# The Literature Collection

X. J. Kennedy • Dana Gioia

*with assistance from Dan Stone*

**PEARSON**

Boston   Columbus   Indianapolis   New York   San Francisco   Upper Saddle River
Amsterdam   Cape Town   Dubai   London   Madrid   Milan   Munich   Paris   Montreal   Toronto
Delhi   Mexico City   São Paulo   Sydney   Hong Kong   Seoul   Singapore   Taipei   Tokyo

Vice President and Editor-in-Chief: Joseph P. Terry
Development Editor: Erin Reilly Jenkins
Senior Supplements Editor: Donna Campion
Text Design and Electronic Page Makeup: Grapevine Publishing Services, Inc.

Instructor Review Access: *The Literature Collection* by X. J. Kennedy and Dana Gioia, with assistance from Dan Stone.

Copyright © 2013 by Pearson Education, Inc.

All rights reserved. Printed in the United States of America. Instructors may reproduce portions of this book for classroom use only. All other reproductions are strictly prohibited without prior permission of the publisher, except in the case of brief quotations embodied in critical articles and reviews.

2 3 4 5 6 7 8 9 10–DOC–14 13

www.pearsonhighered.com

ISBN 10:   0-205-89100-4
ISBN 13: 978-0-205-89100-9

Welcome to a new kind of literature anthology. *The Literature Collection* is an enhanced eText divided into four approximately equal parts—fiction, poetry, drama, and writing. In developing the eText, one of our primary goals was to adopt a design that replicates the very best elements of print while incorporating some of the best elements of other media. While we have striven to protect narrative flow and encourage linear reading, many of the stories, poems and plays are enriched by performances, audio lectures, video, questions, and writing and research resources.

As with our traditional books, *The Literature Collection* introduces college students to the appreciation and experience of literature in its major forms. We also try to help students to think critically and communicate effectively through writing. Both editors of this volume are writers. Our intent has always been to write a book that students will read eagerly and enjoy. In education, it never hurts to have a little fun.

Overall, we have tried to create a book to help readers develop sensitivity to language, culture, and identity, to lead them beyond the boundaries of their own selves, and to see the world through the eyes of others. This book is built on the assumption that great literature can enrich and enlarge the lives it touches.

# A Word About Careers

The ability to read and write well has a decisive impact on the lives of students. As recent studies have repeatedly shown, students who gain proficiency in reading and writing do better in school, the job market, and their later careers. Yet, many students wonder what use literary study is when they really want to focus on their careers. They ask, "Why spend time trying to figure out some hundred-year-old poem when I'm studying to be a nurse or an engineer?", "Why should I puzzle through a story that has no practical application in the real world?", "Why should I care about literature at all?" For those students, we offer this brief explanation of how reading and writing will change the student's life for the better:

Most students agree that to read celebrated writers such as William Faulkner, Emily Dickinson, and William Shakespeare is probably good for the spirit. Most students even take some pleasure in the experience. But many, not planning to teach English and impatient to begin some other career, wonder if the study of literature, however enjoyable, isn't a waste of time—or at least, an annoying obstacle. This objection may seem reasonable at first glance, but it rests on a shaky assumption. Success in a career does not depend merely on learning the specialized information and skills required to join a profession. In most careers, according to one senior business executive, people often fail not because they don't understand their jobs, but because they don't understand their co-workers, their clients, or their customers. They don't ever see the world from another person's point of view. Their problem is a failure of imagination. To leap over the wall of self and to look through another's eyes is valuable experience that literature offers. If you are lucky, you may never meet (or have to do business with) anyone exactly like Mrs. Turpin in the story "Revelation," and yet you will learn much about the kind of person she is from Flannery O'Connor's fictional portrait of her. What is it like to be black, a white may wonder? James Baldwin, Gwendolyn Brooks,

Rita Dove, Langston Hughes, Zora Neale Hurston, Alice Walker, August Wilson, and others have knowledge to impart. What is it like to be a woman? If a man would like to learn, let him read (for a start) Sandra Cisneros, Kate Chopin, Susan Glaspell, Alice Munro, Sylvia Plath, Katherine Anne Porter, Flannery O'Connor, Adrienne Rich, and Amy Tan, and perhaps, too, Henrik Ibsen's *A Doll's House* and John Steinbeck's "The Chrysanthemums." Plodding single-mindedly toward careers, some people are like horses wearing blinders. For many, the goals look fixed and predictable. Competent nurses, accountants, and dental technicians seem always in demand. Others may find that in our society some careers, like waves in the sea, will rise or fall unexpectedly. Think how many professions we now take for granted, which a few years ago didn't even exist: genetic engineering, energy conservation, digital editing, and website design.

Others that once looked like lifetime meal tickets have been cut back and nearly ruined: shoe repairing, commercial fishing, railroading. In a perpetually changing society, it may be risky to lock yourself on one track to a career, refusing to consider any other. "We are moving," writes John Naisbitt in *Megatrends*, a study of our changing society, "from the specialist, soon obsolete, to the generalist who can adapt." Perhaps the greatest opportunity in your whole life lies in a career that has yet to be invented. If you do change your career as you go along, you will be like most people. According to a U.S. Bureau of Labor Statistics survey conducted in September 2010, the average American holds over eleven jobs between the ages of 18 and 44—often completely changing his or her basic occupation. When for some unforeseen reason you have to make such a change, basic skills—and a knowledge of humanity—may be your most valuable credentials.

Literature has much practical knowledge to offer you. An art of words, it can help you become more sensitive to language—both your own and other people's. It can make you aware of the difference between the word that is exactly right and the word that is merely good enough—Mark Twain calls it "the difference between the lightning and the lightning-bug." Read a fine work of literature alertly, and some of its writer's sensitivity to words may grow on you. A Supreme Court Justice, John Paul Stevens, once remarked that the best preparation for law school is to study poetry. Why? George D. Gopen, an English professor with a law degree, says it may be because "no other discipline so closely replicates the central question asked in the study of legal thinking: Here is a text; in how many ways can it have meaning?" Many careers today, besides law, call for close reading and clear writing—as well as careful listening and thoughtful speech. Lately, college placement directors have reported more demand for graduates who are good readers and writers. The reason is evident: Employers need people who can handle words. In a survey conducted by Cornell University, business executives were asked to rank in importance the traits they look for when hiring. Leadership was first, but skill in writing and speaking came in fourth, ahead of both managerial and analytical skills. Times change, but to think cogently and to express yourself well will always be the abilities the world needs.

# Table of Contents

Two Ways to Explore *The Literature Collection* ....................Inside Front Cover

Table of Contents for *The Literature Collection* .................................................1

Tour of *The Literature Collection*
    Tables of Contents: Multiple Paths for Finding Selections ...................37
    The Multimedia Environment ..................................................................42
    MyLiteratureLab .........................................................................................51

Ordering and Assigning *The Literature Collection* for Your Course ...............54

Other Formats .........................................................................................................57

Media Index ............................................................................................................58

Copyright © 2013 by Pearson Education, Inc.

# Table of Contents for The Literature Collection

We have created this eText edition of *Literature* with the simple aim of introducing useful new features only possible in an online environment without losing the best-liked material that has made our print books a trusted resource for 12 editions. Teaching is a kind of conversation between instructor and student and between reader and text. By re-envisioning *Literature*, we help keep this conversation fresh by mixing the classic with the new and the familiar with the unexpected.

You are holding in your hands the equivalent of a 2,500 page book. The *Literature Collection* offers a wide variety of popular and provocative stories, poems, plays, and critical prose—from traditional favorites to exciting and sometimes surprising contemporary selections.

- **More than 80 diverse and exciting stories** from authors new and old from around the globe.
- **514 great poems**, familiar and less well known, mixing classic favorites with engaging contemporary work from a wonderful range of poets.
- **22 plays**—a rich array of drama from classical Greek tragedy to Shakespeare to contemporary work by August Wilson and Anna Deavere Smith.
- **132 critical prose pieces**—extensive selections help students think about different approaches to reading, interpreting, and writing about literature.
- **Nine casebooks on major authors and literary masterpieces** —provide students with a variety of material, including biographies, photographs, critical commentaries, and author statements, to begin an in-depth study of writers and works frequently used for critical analyses or research papers.

*The Literature Collections* includes eight writing chapters that provide comprehensive coverage of the composition and research process, including up-to-date MLA coverage. The text closes with Chapter 48, *Critical Approaches to Literature*, which includes pieces for every major critical school, carefully chosen both to illustrate the major theoretical approaches and to be accessible to beginning students.

# Brief Table of Contents

 ## FICTION

| | |
|---|---|
| 1 | Reading a Story |
| 2 | Point of View |
| 3 | Character |
| 4 | Setting |
| 5 | Tone and Style |
| 6 | Theme |
| 7 | Symbol |
| 8 | Reading Long Stories and Novels |
| 9 | Latin American Fiction |
| 10 | Two Critical Casebooks: Edgar Allan Poe and Flannery O'Connor |
| 11 | Critical Casebook: Two Stories in Depth |
| 12 | Stories for Further Reading |

# POETRY

13  Reading a Poem
14  Listening to a Voice
15  Words
16  Saying and Suggesting
17  Imagery
18  Figures of Speech
19  Song
20  Sound
21  Rhythm
22  Closed Form
23  Open Form
24  Symbol
25  Myth and Narrative
26  Poetry and Personal Identity
27  Translation
28  Poetry in Spanish: Literature of Latin America
29  Recognizing Excellence
30  What is Poetry?
31  Two Critical Casebooks: Emily Dickinson and Langston Hughes
32  Critical Casebook: T. S. Eliot's "The Love Song of J. Alfred Prufrock"
33  Poems for Further Reading

## DRAMA

34  Reading a Play
35  Modes of Drama: Tragedy and Comedy
36  Critical Casebook: Sophocles
37  Critical Casebook: Shakespeare
38  The Modern Theater
39  Evaluating a Play
40  Plays for Further Reading

## WRITING

41  Writing About Literature
42  Writing About a Story
43  Writing About a Poem
44  Writing About a Play
45  Writing a Research Paper
46  Writing as Discovery: Keeping a Journal
47  Writing an Essay Exam
48  Critical Approaches to Literature

# Detailed Table of Contents

## ▶ FICTION

Talking with *Amy Tan*   1

### 1  Reading a Story   3

THE ART OF FICTION   3
TYPES OF SHORT FICTION   4
    W. Somerset Maugham, The Appointment in Samarra   5
    Aesop, The Fox and the Grapes   6
    Bidpai, The Camel and His Friends   7
    Chuang Tzu, Independence   9
    Jakob and Wilhelm Grimm, Godfather Death   11
PLOT   12
THE SHORT STORY   13
    John Updike, A & P   14
WRITING EFFECTIVELY
    John Updike on Writing, Why Write?   15
        THINKING ABOUT PLOT   16

### 2  Point of View   17

IDENTIFYING POINT OF VIEW   18
TYPES OF NARRATORS   19
STREAM OF CONSCIOUSNESS   20
    ZZ Packer, Brownies   21
    Eudora Welty, A Worn Path   22
    James Baldwin, Sonny's Blues   23
WRITING EFFECTIVELY
    James Baldwin on Writing, Race and the African American Writer   24
        THINKING ABOUT POINT OF VIEW   25

### 3  Character   26

TYPES OF CHARACTERS   27
    Katherine Anne Porter, The Jilting of Granny Weatherall   28
    Nathaniel Hawthorne, Young Goodman Brown   29
    Katherine Mansfield, Miss Brill   30
    Raymond Carver, Cathedral   31

WRITING EFFECTIVELY
    Raymond Carver on Writing, Commonplace but Precise Language   32
        THINKING ABOUT CHARACTER   33

## 4  Setting   34

ELEMENTS OF SETTING   34
HISTORICAL FICTION   35
REGIONALISM   36
NATURALISM   37
    Kate Chopin, The Storm   38
    Jack London, To Build a Fire   39
    Ray Bradbury, A Sound of Thunder   40
    Amy Tan, A Pair of Tickets   41
WRITING EFFECTIVELY
    Amy Tan on Writing, Setting the Voice   42
        THINKING ABOUT SETTING   43

## 5  Tone and Style   44

TONE   45
STYLE   46
DICTION   47
    Ernest Hemingway, A Clean, Well-Lighted Place   48
IRONY   49
    O. Henry, The Gift of the Magi   50
    Anne Tyler, Teenage Wasteland   51
WRITING EFFECTIVELY
    Ernest Hemingway on Writing, The Direct Style   52
        THINKING ABOUT TONE AND STYLE   53

## 6  Theme   54

PLOT VERSUS THEME   55
THEME AS A UNIFYING DEVICE   56
FINDING THE THEME   57
    Stephen Crane, The Open Boat   58
    Alice Munro, How I Met My Husband   59
    Luke 15:11–32, The Parable of the Prodigal Son   60
    Kurt Vonnegut Jr., Harrison Bergeron   61
WRITING EFFECTIVELY
    Kurt Vonnegut Jr. on Writing, The Themes of Science Fiction   62
        THINKING ABOUT THEME   63

## 7 Symbol  64

ALLEGORY  65
SYMBOLS  66
RECOGNIZING SYMBOLS  67
- John Steinbeck, The Chrysanthemums  68
- John Cheever, The Swimmer  69
- Ursula K. Le Guin, The Ones Who Walk Away from Omelas  70
- Shirley Jackson, The Lottery  71

WRITING EFFECTIVELY
- Shirley Jackson on Writing, Biography of a Story  72
  - THINKING ABOUT SYMBOLS  73

## 8 Reading Long Stories and Novels  74

ORIGINS OF THE NOVEL  75
NOVELISTIC METHODS  76
READING NOVELS  77
- Leo Tolstoy, The Death of Ivan Ilych  78
- Franz Kafka, The Metamorphosis  90

WRITING EFFECTIVELY
- Franz Kafka on Writing, Discussing *The Metamorphosis*  93
  - THINKING ABOUT LONG STORIES AND NOVELS  94

## 9 Latin American Fiction  95

"EL BOOM"  96
MAGIC REALISM  97
AFTER THE BOOM  98
- Jorge Luis Borges, The Gospel According to Mark  99
- Gabriel García Márquez, A Very Old Man with Enormous Wings  100
- Isabel Allende, The Judge's Wife  101
- Inés Arredondo, The Shunammite  102

WRITING EFFECTIVELY
- Gabriel García Márquez on Writing, My Beginnings as a Writer  103

## 10 Two Critical Casebooks: Edgar Allan Poe and Flannery O'Connor  104

**EDGAR ALLAN POE**  105
- The Tell-Tale Heart  105
- The Cask of Amontillado  106
- The Fall of the House of Usher  107

EDGAR ALLAN POE ON WRITING  108

Copyright © 2013 by Pearson Education, Inc.

        The Tale and Its Effect   108
        On Imagination   109
        The Philosophy of Composition   110
    CRITICS ON EDGAR ALLAN POE   111
        Daniel Hoffman, The Father-Figure in "The Tell-Tale Heart"   111
        Robert Louis Stevenson, Costume in "The Cask of Amontillado"   112
        Elena V. Baraban, The Motive for Murder in "The Cask of Amontillado"   113
        Charles Baudelaire, Poe's Characters   114
        James Tuttleton, Poe's Protagonists and the Ideal World   115
        Carl Mowery, Madness in Poe's "The Fall of the House of Usher"   116

**FLANNERY O'CONNOR**   117
        A Good Man Is Hard to Find   117
        Revelation   118
        Parker's Back   119
    FLANNERY O'CONNOR ON WRITING   120
        From "On Her Own Work"   120
        On Her Catholic Faith   121
        From "The Grotesque in Southern Fiction"   122
    CRITICS ON FLANNERY O'CONNOR
        J. O. Tate, A Good Source Is Not So Hard to Find: The Real Life Misfit   123
        Louise S. Cowan, The Character of Mrs. Turpin in "Revelation"   124
        Dean Flower, Listening to Flannery O'Connor   125

## 11 Critical Casebook: Two Stories in Depth   126

    **CHARLOTTE PERKINS GILMAN**   127
        The Yellow Wallpaper   127
    CHARLOTTE PERKINS GILMAN ON WRITING   128
        Why I Wrote "The Yellow Wallpaper"   128
        Whatever Is   129
        The Nervous Breakdown of Women   130
    CRITICS ON "THE YELLOW WALLPAPER"   131
        Sandra M. Gilbert and Susan Gubar, Imprisonment and Escape: The Psychology of Confinement   131
        Elizabeth Ammons, Biographical Echoes in "The Yellow Wallpaper"   132

    **ALICE WALKER**   133
        Everyday Use   133

ALICE WALKER ON WRITING   134
    The Black Woman Writer in America   134
    Reflections on Writing and Women's Lives   135
CRITICS ON "EVERYDAY USE"   136
    Barbara T. Christian, "Everyday Use" and the Black Power Movement   136
    Mary Helen Washington, "Everyday Use" as a Portrait of the Artist   137
    Houston A. Baker and Charlotte Pierce-Baker, Stylish vs. Sacred in "Everyday Use"   138
    Elaine Showalter, Quilt as Metaphor in "Everyday Use"   139

# 12   Stories for Further Reading   140

    Chinua Achebe, Dead Men's Path   141
    Sherwood Anderson, Hands   142
    Margaret Atwood, Happy Endings   143
    Toni Cade Bambara, The Lesson (See Chapter 47)
    Ambrose Bierce, An Occurrence at Owl Creek Bridge   144
    T. Coraghessan Boyle, Greasy Lake   145
    Willa Cather, Paul's Case   146
    Anton Chekov, An Upheaval   147
    Anton Chekov, Misery   148
    Kate Chopin, The Story of an Hour   149
    Kate Chopin, Désirée's Baby   150
    Sandra Cisneros, The House on Mango Street   151
    Joseph Conrad, The Secret Sharer   152
    Arthur Conan Doyle, The Adventure of the Speckled Band   154
    Ralph Ellison, Battle Royal   155
    Gustav Flaubert, A Simple Heart   156
    Charlotte Perkins Gilman, The Unnatural Mother   161
    Susan Glaspell, A Jury of Her Peers   162
    Nikolai Gogol, The Overcoat   163
    Nathaniel Hawthorne, The Birthmark   164
    Zora Neale Hurston, Sweat   165
    James Joyce, Araby   166
    James Joyce, Eveline   167
    James Joyce, The Dead   168
    Franz Kafka, Before the Law   171
    Jamaica Kincaid, Girl   172
    Jhumpa Lahiri, Interpreter of Maladies   173
    D. H. Lawrence, The Rocking-Horse Winner   174
    D. H. Lawrence, Odour of Chrysanthemums   175

David Leavitt, A Place I've Never Been    176
Naguib Mahfouz, The Lawsuit    177
Katherine Mansfield, The Garden-Party    178
Bobbie Ann Mason, Shiloh    179
Guy de Maupassant, Mother Savage    180
Guy de Maupassant, The Necklace (see page 1221)
Herman Melville, Bartleby, the Scrivener    181
Joyce Carol Oates, Where Are You Going, Where Have You Been?    183
Tim O'Brien, The Things They Carried    184
Daniel Orozco, Orientation    185
Robert Louis Stevenson, The Bottle Imp    186
Edith Wharton, The Other Two    187
Oscar Wilde, The Happy Prince    188
Tobias Wolff, The Rich Brother    189
Virginia Woolf, A Haunted House    190

▶ **POETRY**

Talking with *Kay Ryan*    191

## 13  Reading a Poem    194

POETRY OR VERSE    195
READING A POEM    196
PARAPHRASE    197
    William Butler Yeats, The Lake Isle of Innisfree    198
LYRIC POETRY    199
    Robert Hayden, Those Winter Sundays    200
    Adrienne Rich, Aunt Jennifer's Tigers    201
NARRATIVE POETRY    202
    Anonymous, Sir Patrick Spence    203
    Robert Frost, "Out, Out—"    204
DRAMATIC POETRY    205
    Robert Browning, My Last Duchess    206
DIDACTIC POETRY    207
WRITING EFFECTIVELY
    Adrienne Rich on Writing, Recalling "Aunt Jennifer's Tigers"    208
        THINKING ABOUT PARAPHRASING    209
    William Stafford, Ask Me    209
    William Stafford, A Paraphrase of "Ask Me"    209

# 14 Listening to a Voice 210

TONE 210
    Theodore Roethke, My Papa's Waltz 211
    Countee Cullen, For a Lady I Know 212
    Anne Bradstreet, The Author to Her Book 214
    Walt Whitman, To a Locomotive in Winter 215
    Emily Dickinson, I like to see it lap the Miles 216
    Benjamin Alire Sáenz, To the Desert 217
    Gwendolyn Brooks, Speech to the Young. Speech to the Progress-Toward 218
    Weldon Kees, For My Daughter 219

THE PERSON IN THE POEM 220
    Natasha Trethewey, White Lies 221
    Edwin Arlington Robinson, Luke Havergal 223
    Anonymous, Dog Haiku 224
    William Wordsworth, I Wandered Lonely as a Cloud 225
    Dorothy Wordsworth, Journal Entry 225
    James Stephens, A Glass of Beer 227
    Anne Sexton, Her Kind 228
    William Carlos Williams, The Red Wheelbarrow 229

IRONY 230
    Robert Creeley, Oh No 231
    W. H. Auden, The Unknown Citizen 233
    Sharon Olds, Rite of Passage 234
    Julie Sheehan, Hate Poem 235
    Sarah N. Cleghorn, The Golf Links 236
    Edna St. Vincent Millay, Second Fig 237
    Thomas Hardy, The Workbox 238

FOR REVIEW AND FURTHER STUDY 239
    William Blake, The Chimney Sweeper 239
    William Jay Smith, American Primitive 240
    David Lehman, Rejection Slip 241
    William Stafford, At the Un-National Monument Along the Canadian Border 242
    Richard Lovelace, To Lucasta 243
    Wilfred Owen, Dulce et Decorum Est 244

WRITING EFFECTIVELY
    Wilfred Owen on Writing, War Poetry 245
        THINKING ABOUT TONE 246

## 15 Words 247

LITERAL MEANING: WHAT A POEM SAYS FIRST 247
   William Carlos Williams, This Is Just to Say 248
DICTION 249
   Robert Graves, Down, Wanton, Down! 250
   John Donne, Batter my heart, three-personed God, for You 251
THE VALUE OF A DICTIONARY 252
   Henry Wadsworth Longfellow, Aftermath 253
   Kay Ryan, Mockingbird 254
   J. V. Cunningham, Friend, on this scaffold Thomas More lies dead 256
   Samuel Menashe, Bread 257
   Carl Sandburg, Grass 258
WORD CHOICE AND WORD ORDER 259
   Robert Herrick, Upon Julia's Clothes 260
   Kay Ryan, Blandeur 261
   Thomas Hardy, The Ruined Maid 262
   Richard Eberhart, The Fury of Aerial Bombardment 263
   Wendy Cope, Lonely Hearts 264
FOR REVIEW AND FURTHER STUDY 265
   E. E. Cummings, anyone lived in a pretty how town 265
   Billy Collins, The Names 266
   Christian Wiman, When the Time's Toxins 267
   Anonymous, Carnation Milk 268
   Gina Valdés, English con Salsa 269
   Lewis Carroll, Jabberwocky 270
WRITING EFFECTIVELY
   Lewis Carroll, Humpty Dumpty Explicates "Jabberwocky" 271
      THINKING ABOUT DICTION 272

## 16 Saying and Suggesting 273

DENOTATION AND CONNOTATION 274
   John Masefield, Cargoes 275
   William Blake, London 276
   Wallace Stevens, Disillusionment of Ten O'Clock 277
   Gwendolyn Brooks, The Bean Eaters 278
   E. E. Cummings, next to of course god america i 279
   Robert Frost, Fire and Ice 280
   Timothy Steele, Epitaph 281
   Diane Thiel, The Minefield 282

Detailed Table of Contents   13

    H.D., Storm   283
    Alfred, Lord Tennyson, Tears, Idle Tears   284
    Richard Wilbur, Love Calls Us to the Things of This World   285
WRITING EFFECTIVELY
    Richard Wilbur on Writing, Concerning "Love Calls Us to the
    Things Of This World"   286
        THINKING ABOUT DENOTATION AND CONNOTATION   287

# 17   Imagery   288

    Ezra Pound, In a Station of the Metro   288
    Taniguchi Buson, The piercing chill I feel   289
IMAGERY   290
    T. S. Eliot, The winter evening settles down   291
    Theodore Roethke, Root Cellar   292
    Elizabeth Bishop, The Fish   293
    Charles Simic, Fork   294
    Emily Dickinson, A Route of Evanescence   295
    Jean Toomer, Reapers   296
    Gerard Manley Hopkins, Pied Beauty   297
ABOUT HAIKU   298
    Arakida Moritake, The falling flower   298
    Matsuo Basho, Heat-lightning streak   299
    Matsuo Basho, In the old stone pool   299
    Taniguchi Buson, On the one-ton temple bell   299
    Taniguchi Buson, Moonrise on mudflats   299
    Kobayashi Issa, only one guy   299
    Kobayashi Issa, Cricket   299
HAIKU FROM JAPANESE INTERNMENT CAMPS   300
    Suiko Matsushita, Rain shower from mountain   300
    Suiko Matsushita, Cosmos in bloom   300
    Hakuro Wada, Even the croaking of frogs   300
    Neiji Ozawa, The war—this year   300
CONTEMPORARY HAIKU   301
    Etheridge Knight, Making jazz swing in   301
    Gary Snyder, After weeks of watching the roof leak   301
    Penny Harter, broken bowl   301
    Jennifer Brutschy, Born Again   301
    Adelle Foley, Learning to Shave   301
    Garry Gay, Hole in the ozone   301

Copyright © 2013 by Pearson Education, Inc.

FOR REVIEW AND FURTHER STUDY   302
    John Keats, Bright star! would I were steadfast as thou art   302
    Walt Whitman, The Runner   303
    H.D., Oread   304
    William Carlos Williams, El Hombre   305
    Robert Bly, Driving to Town Late to Mail a Letter   306
    Billy Collins, Embrace   307
    Chana Bloch, Tired Sex   308
    Gary Snyder, Mid-August at Sourdough Mountain Lookout   309
    Kevin Prufer, Pause, Pause   310
    Stevie Smith, Not Waving but Drowning   311
WRITING EFFECTIVELY
    Ezra Pound on Writing, The Image   312
        THINKING ABOUT IMAGERY   313

## 18  Figures of Speech   314

WHY SPEAK FIGURATIVELY?   314
    Alfred, Lord Tennyson, The Eagle   315
    William Shakespeare, Shall I compare thee to a summer's day?   316
METAPHOR AND SIMILE   317
    Emily Dickinson, My Life had stood – a Loaded Gun   318
    Alfred, Lord Tennyson, Flower in the Crannied Wall   319
    William Blake, To see a world in a grain of sand   319
    Sylvia Plath, Metaphors   320
    Emily Dickinson, It dropped so low – in my Regard   321
    Jill Alexander Essbaum, The Heart   322
OTHER FIGURES OF SPEECH   323
    James Stephens, The Wind   324
    Robinson Jeffers, Hands   325
    Margaret Atwood, You fit into me   327
    George Herbert, The Pulley   328
    Dana Gioia, Money   329
    Carl Sandburg, Fog   330
    Charles Simic, My Shoes   331
FOR REVIEW AND FURTHER STUDY
    Robert Frost, The Silken Tent   332
    Jane Kenyon, The Suitor   333
    Robert Frost, The Secret Sits   334
    A. R. Ammons, Coward   335

Kay Ryan, Turtle    336
April Lindner, Low Tide    337
Emily Brontë, Love and Friendship    338
Robert Burns, Oh, my love is like a red, red rose    339
**WRITING EFFECTIVELY**
Robert Frost on Writing, The Importance of Poetic Metaphor    340
THINKING ABOUT METAPHORS    341

# 19  Song    342

SINGING AND SAYING    342
Ben Jonson, To Celia    343
James Weldon Johnson, Sence You Went Away    344
William Shakespeare, Fear no more the heat o' the sun    345
Edwin Arlington Robinson, Richard Cory    347
Paul Simon, Richard Cory    348
BALLADS    349
Anonymous, Bonny Barbara Allan    350
Dudley Randall, Ballad of Birmingham    352
BLUES    353
Bessie Smith with Clarence Williams, Jailhouse Blues    354
W. H. Auden, Funeral Blues    355
Kevin Young, Late Blues    356
RAP    357
FOR REVIEW AND FURTHER STUDY    358
Bob Dylan, The Times They Are a-Changin'    358
Aimee Mann, Deathly    359
**WRITING EFFECTIVELY**
Bob Dylan on Writing, The Term "Protest Singer" Didn't Exist    360
THINKING ABOUT POETRY AND SONG    361

# 20  Sound    362

SOUND AS MEANING    362
Alexander Pope, True Ease in Writing comes from Art, not Chance    363
William Butler Yeats, Who Goes with Fergus?    364
John Updike, Recital    365
William Wordsworth, A Slumber Did My Spirit Seal    366
Aphra Behn, When maidens are young    367
ALLITERATION AND ASSONANCE    368
A. E. Housman, Eight O'Clock    369

16   Detailed Table of Contents

      James Joyce, All day I hear   370
      Alfred, Lord Tennyson, The splendor falls on castle walls   371
  RIME   372
      William Cole, On my boat on Lake Cayuga   373
      Hilaire Belloc, The Hippopotamus   375
      Bob Kaufman, No More Jazz at Alcatraz   376
      William Butler Yeats, Leda and the Swan   378
      Gerard Manley Hopkins, God's Grandeur   379
      Robert Frost, Desert Places   380
  READING AND HEARING POEMS ALOUD   381
      Michael Stillman, In Memoriam John Coltrane   382
      William Shakespeare, Hark, hark, the lark   383
      Kevin Young, Doo Wop   384
        THINKING ABOUT A POEM'S SOUND   385

## 21  Rhythm   386

  STRESSES AND PAUSES   386
      Gwendolyn Brooks, We Real Cool   387
      Alfred, Lord Tennyson, Break, Break, Break   388
      Ben Jonson, Slow, slow, fresh fount, keep time with my salt tears   389
      Dorothy Parker, Résumé   390
  METER   391
      Edna St. Vincent Millay, Counting-out Rhyme   392
      Edith Sitwell, Mariner Man   393
      A. E. Housman, When I was one-and-twenty   394
      William Carlos Williams, Smell!   395
      Walt Whitman, Beat! Beat! Drums!   396
      David Mason, Song of the Powers   397
      Langston Hughes, Dream Boogie   398
  WRITING EFFECTIVELY
      Gwendolyn Brooks on Writing, Hearing "We Real Cool"   399
        THINKING ABOUT RHYTHM   400

## 22  Closed Form   401

  FORMAL PATTERNS   402
      John Keats, This living hand, now warm and capable   402
      Robert Graves, Counting the Beats   406
      John Donne, Song   407
      Phillis Levin, Brief Bio   409

Copyright © 2013 by Pearson Education, Inc.

THE SONNET   411
    William Shakespeare, Let me not to the marriage of true minds   412
    Michael Drayton, Since there's no help, come let us kiss and part   413
THE ITALIAN SONNET   414
    Edna St. Vincent Millay, What lips my lips have kissed, and where, and why   415
    Robert Frost, Acquainted with the Night   416
CONTEMPORARY SONNETS   417
    Kim Addonizio, First Poem for You   418
    Mark Jarman, Unholy Sonnet: After the Praying   419
    A. E. Stallings, Sine Qua Non   420
    Amit Majmudar, Rites to Allay the Dead   421
    R. S. Gwynn, Shakespearean Sonnet   422
THE EPIGRAM   423
    Sir John Harrington, Of Treason   424
    William Blake, To H—   425
    Langston Hughes, Two Somewhat Different Epigrams   426
    Dorothy Parker, The Actress   427
    John Frederick Nims, Contemplation   428
    Hilaire Belloc, Fatigue   429
    Wendy Cope, Variation on Belloc's "Fatigue"   430
POETWEETS   432
    Lawrence Bridges, Two Poetweets   432
    Robert Pinsky, Low Pay Piecework   432
OTHER FORMS   433
    Dylan Thomas, Do not go gentle into that good night   434
    Robert Bridges, Triolet   435
    Elizabeth Bishop, Sestina   436
WRITING EFFECTIVELY
    A. E. Stallings on Writing, On Form and Artifice   437
        THINKING ABOUT A SONNET   438

## 23 Open Form   439

    Denise Levertov, Ancient Stairway   440
FREE VERSE   441
    E. E. Cummings, Buffalo Bill 's   442
    W. S. Merwin, For the Anniversary of My Death   443
    William Carlos Williams, The Dance   444
    Stephen Crane, The Wayfarer   445

        Walt Whitman, Cavalry Crossing a Ford   446
        Ezra Pound, The Garden   447
        Wallace Stevens, Thirteen Ways of Looking at a Blackbird   449
PROSE POETRY   450
        Charles Simic, The Magic Study of Happiness   451
        Joy Harjo, Mourning Song   452
VISUAL POETRY   453
        George Herbert, Easter Wings   453
        John Hollander, Swan and Shadow   454
CONCRETE POETRY   456
        Richard Kostelanetz, Ramón Gómez de la Serna, Simultaneous Translations   456
        Dorthi Charles, Concrete Cat   457
FOR REVIEW AND FURTHER STUDY   458
        E. E. Cummings, in Just-   458
        Francisco X. Alarcón, Frontera / Border   459
        Carole Satyamurti, I Shall Paint My Nails Red   460
        David St. John, Hush   461
        Alice Fulton, What I Like   462
WRITING EFFECTIVELY
        Walt Whitman on Writing, The Poetry of the Future   463
        THINKING ABOUT FREE VERSE   464

# 24 Symbol   465

THE MEANINGS OF A SYMBOL   466
        T. S. Eliot, The Boston Evening Transcript   467
        Emily Dickinson, The Lightning is a yellow Fork   468
THE SYMBOLIST MOVEMENT   469
IDENTIFYING SYMBOLS   470
        Thomas Hardy, Neutral Tones   471
ALLEGORY   472
        Matthew 13:24–30, The Parable of the Good Seed   473
        George Herbert, Redemption   474
        Edwin Markham, Outwitted   475
        Suji Kwock Kim, Occupation   476
        Robert Frost, The Road Not Taken   478
        Antonio Machado, Proverbios y Cantares (XXIX)   479
        Translated by Michael Ortiz, 1912 Traveler   479
        Christina Rossetti, Uphill   480

FOR REVIEW AND FURTHER STUDY   481
    William Carlos Williams, The Young Housewife   481
    Ted Kooser, Carrie   482
    Mary Oliver, Wild Geese   483
    Tami Haaland, Lipstick   484
    Lorine Niedecker, Popcorn-can cover   485
    Wallace Stevens, The Snow Man   486
    Wallace Stevens, Anecdote of the Jar   487
WRITING EFFECTIVELY
    William Butler Yeats on Writing, Poetic Symbols   488
        THINKING ABOUT SYMBOLS   489

## 25 Myth and Narrative   490

ORIGINS OF MYTH   491
    Robert Frost, Nothing Gold Can Stay   492
    William Wordsworth, The world is too much with us   493
    H.D., Helen   494
    Edgar Allan Poe, To Helen   495
ARCHETYPE   496
    Louise Bogan, Medusa   497
    John Keats, La Belle Dame sans Merci   498
PERSONAL MYTH   499
    William Butler Yeats, The Second Coming   500
    Gregory Orr, Two Lines from the Brothers Grimm   501
MYTH AND POPULAR CULTURE   502
    A. E. Stallings, First Love: A Quiz   504
    Anne Sexton, Cinderella   505
WRITING EFFECTIVELY
    Anne Sexton on Writing, Transforming Fairy Tales   506
        THINKING ABOUT MYTH   507

## 26 Poetry and Personal Identity   508

CONFESSIONAL POETRY   509
    Sylvia Plath, Lady Lazarus   510
IDENTITY POETICS   512
    Rhina Espaillat, Bilingual/Bilingüe   513
CULTURE, RACE, AND ETHNICITY   514
    Claude McKay, America   515
    Shirley Geok-lin Lim, Riding into California   517

Francisco X. Alarcón, The X in My Name   518
Judith Ortiz Cofer, Quinceañera   519
Sherman Alexie, The Powwow at the End of the World   520
Yusef Komunyakaa, Facing It   521

GENDER   522
Anne Stevenson, Sous-entendu   523
Carolyn Kizer, Bitch   524
Rafael Campo, For J. W.   525
Donald Justice, Men at Forty   526
Adrienne Rich, Women   527

FOR REVIEW AND FURTHER STUDY   528
Brian Turner, The Hurt Locker   528
Katha Pollitt, Mind-Body Problem   529
Andrew Hudgins, Elegy for My Father, Who Is Not Dead   530

WRITING EFFECTIVELY
Rhina Espaillat on Writing, Being a Bilingual Writer   531
THINKING ABOUT POETIC VOICE AND IDENTITY   532

# 27 Translation   533

IS POETIC TRANSLATION POSSIBLE?   533
WORLD POETRY   534
Li Po, Drinking Alone Beneath the Moon (Chinese text)   535
Li Po, Yue Xia Du Zhoe (phonetic Chinese transcription)   535
Translated by Arthur Waley, Drinking Alone by Moonlight   535

COMPARING TRANSLATIONS   536
Horace, "Carpe Diem" Ode (Latin text)   536
Horace, "Carpe Diem" Ode (literal translation)   536
Translated by Edwin Arlington Robinson, Horace to Leuconoë   536
Translated by A. E. Stallings, A New Year's Toast   536

TRANSLATING FORM   537
Omar Khayyam, Rubai XII (Persian text)   537
Omar Khayyam, Rubai XII (literal translation)   537
Translated by Edward FitzGerald, A Book of Verses underneath the Bough   537
Translated by Dick Davis, I Need a Bare Sufficiency   537
Omar Khayyam, Rubaiyat   537
Translated by Edward FitzGerald, Come, fill the Cup, and in the fire of Spring   537

Translated by Edward FitzGerald, Some for the Glories of this World   537
Translated by Edward FitzGerald, The Moving Finger writes   537
Translated by Edward FitzGerald, Ah Love! could you and I with Him conspire   537

PARODY   538
   Anonymous, We four lads from Liverpool are   538
   Hugh Kingsmill, What, still alive at twenty-two?   539
   Andrea Paterson, Because I could not Dump   540
   Harryette Mullen, Dim Lady   541
   Gene Fehler, If Richard Lovelace Became a Free Agent   542
   Aaron Abeyta, thirteen ways of looking at a tortilla   543

WRITING EFFECTIVELY
   Arthur Waley on Writing, The Method of Translation   544
      THINKING ABOUT PARODY   545

# 28 Poetry in Spanish: Literature of Latin America   546

   Sor Juana, Presente en que el Cariño Hace Regalo la Llaneza   547
   Translated by Diane Thiel, A Simple Gift Made Rich by Affection   547
   Pablo Neruda, Muchos Somos   548
   Translated by Alastair Reid, We Are Many   548
   Jorge Luis Borges, On his blindness   549
   Translated by Robert Mezey, On His Blindness   549
   Octavio Paz, Con los ojos cerrados   550
   Translated by Eliot Weinberger, With eyes closed   550

SURREALISM IN LATIN AMERICAN POETRY   551
   Frida Kahlo, The Two Fridas   551
   César Vallejo, La cólera que quiebra al hombre en niños   552
   Translated by Thomas Merton, Anger   552

CONTEMPORARY MEXICAN POETRY   553
   José Emilio Pacheco, Alta Traición   553
   Translated by Alastair Reid, High Treason   553
   Pedro Serrano, Golondrinas   554
   Translated by Anna Crowe, Swallows   554
   Tedi López Mills, Convalecencia   555
   Translated by Cheryl Clark, Convalescence   555

WRITING EFFECTIVELY
   Alastair Reid on Writing, Translating Neruda   556

## 29 Recognizing Excellence 557

    Anonymous, O Moon, when I gaze on thy beautiful face 558
    Emily Dickinson, A Dying Tiger – moaned for Drink 559
SENTIMENTALITY 560
    William Stafford, Traveling Through the Dark 561
RECOGNIZING EXCELLENCE 562
    William Butler Yeats, Sailing to Byzantium 563
    Arthur Guiterman, On the Vanity of Earthly Greatness 564
    Percy Bysshe Shelley, Ozymandias 565
    Robert Hayden, Frederick Douglass 567
    Elizabeth Bishop, One Art 568
    John Keats, Ode to a Nightingale 569
    Walt Whitman, O Captain! My Captain! 571
    Dylan Thomas, In My Craft or Sullen Art 573
    Paul Laurence Dunbar, We Wear the Mask 574
    Emma Lazarus, The New Colossus 575
    Edgar Allan Poe, Annabel Lee 576
WRITING EFFECTIVELY
    Edgar Allan Poe on Writing, A Long Poem Does Not Exist 577
        THINKING ABOUT EVALUATING A POEM 578

## 30 What Is Poetry? 579

    Archibald MacLeish, Ars Poetica 579
SOME DEFINITIONS OF POETRY 580
    Dante, Samuel Johnson, Samuel Taylor Coleridge, William Wordsworth, Thomas Hardy, Emily Dickinson, Gerard Manley Hopkins, Robert Frost, Wallace Stevens, Mina Loy, T. S. Eliot, W. H. Auden, José Garcia Villa, Christopher Fry, Elizabeth Bishop, Joy Harjo, Octavio Paz, DeniseLevertov, Lucille Clifton, Charles Simic 580

## 31 Two Critical Casebooks: Emily Dickinson and Langston Hughes 581

**EMILY DICKINSON 582**
    Success is counted sweetest 582
    I taste a liquor never brewed 583
    Wild Nights – Wild Nights! 584
    I felt a Funeral, in my Brain 584
    I'm Nobody! Who are you? 586
    The Soul selects her own Society 587

Some keep the Sabbath going to Church   588
After great pain, a formal feeling comes   589
Much Madness is divinest Sense   590
This is my letter to the World   591
I heard a Fly buzz – when I died   592
Because I could not stop for Death   593
Tell all the Truth but tell it slant   594
There is no Frigate like a Book   595
EMILY DICKINSON ON EMILY DICKINSON   596
Recognizing Poetry   596
Self-Description   597
CRITICS ON EMILY DICKINSON   598
Thomas Wentworth Higginson, Meeting Emily Dickinson   598
Thomas H. Johnson, The Discovery of Emily Dickinson's Manuscripts   599
Richard Wilbur, The Three Privations of Emily Dickinson   600
Cynthia Griffin Wolff, Dickinson and Death (A Reading of "Because I could not stop for Death")   601
Judith Farr, A Reading of "My Life had stood – a Loaded Gun"   602
Sandra M. Gilbert and Susan Gubar, The Freedom of Emily Dickinson   603

**LANGSTON HUGHES   604**
The Negro Speaks of Rivers   604
My People   605
Mother to Son   606
Dream Variations   607
I, Too   608
The Weary Blues   609
Song for a Dark Girl   610
Prayer   611
Ballad of the Landlord   612
Theme for English B   613
Nightmare Boogie   614
Harlem [Dream Deferred]   615
Homecoming   616
LANGSTON HUGHES ON WRITING   617
The Negro Artist and the Racial Mountain   617
The Harlem Renaissance   618
CRITICS ON LANGSTON HUGHES   619
Arnold Rampersad, Hughes as an Experimentalist   619

Rita Dove and Marilyn Nelson, The Voices in Langston Hughes   620
Darryl Pinckney, Black Identity in Langston Hughes   621
Peter Townsend, Langston Hughes and Jazz   622
FURTHER READING   623

## 32 Critical Casebook: T. S. Eliot's "The Love Song of J. Alfred Prufrock"   624

T. S. ELIOT   625
   The Love Song of J. Alfred Prufrock   625
PUBLISHING "PRUFROCK"   626
THE REVIEWERS ON PRUFROCK   627
   Unsigned Review, from Times Literary Supplement   627
   Unsigned Review, from Literary World   628
   Conrad Aiken, from "Divers Realists," The Dial   629
   Babette Deutsch, from "Another Impressionist," The New Republic   630
   Marianne Moore, from "A Note on T. S. Eliot's Book," Poetry   631
   May Sinclair, from "Prufrock and Other Observations: A Criticism," The Little Review   632
T. S. ELIOT ON WRITING   633
   Poetry and Emotion   633
   The Objective Correlative   634
CRITICS ON "PRUFROCK"   635
   Denis Donoghue, One of the Irrefutable Poets   635
   Christopher Ricks, What's in a Name?   636
   Maud Ellmann, Will There Be Time?   637
   Burton Raffel, "Indeterminacy" in Eliot's Poetry   638
   John Berryman, Prufrock's Dilemma   639
   M. L. Rosenthal, Adolescents Singing   640

## 33 Poems for Further Reading   641

Anonymous, Lord Randall   642
Anonymous, The Three Ravens   643
Anonymous, Last Words of the Prophet   644
Anonymous, The Twa Corbies   645
Matthew Arnold, Dover Beach   646
John Ashbery, At North Farm   647
Margaret Atwood, Siren Song   648
W. H. Auden, As I Walked Out One Evening   649
W. H. Auden, Musée des Beaux Arts   650

Jimmy Santiago Baca, Spliced Wire   651
Aphra Behn, A Thousand Martyrs   652
Elizabeth Bishop, Filling Station   653
William Blake, A Poison Tree   654
William Blake, Garden of Love   655
William Blake, The Tyger   656
William Blake, The Sick Rose   657
Anne Bradstreet, To My Dear and Loving Husband   658
Gwendolyn Brooks, The Mother   659
Gwendolyn Brooks, The Rites for Cousin Vit   660
Elizabeth Barrett Browning, Grief   661
Elizabeth Barrett Browning, How Do I Love Thee? Let Me Count the Ways   662
Robert Browning, Porphyria's Lover   663
Robert Browning, Soliloquy of the Spanish Cloister   664
Charles Bukowski, Dostoevsky   665
George Gordon, Lord Byron, When We Two Parted   666
George Gordon, Lord Byron, The Ocean   667
George Gordon, Lord Byron, So We'll Go No More A-Roving   668
Lewis Carroll, The Walrus and the Carpenter   669
Lorna Dee Cervantes, Cannery Town in August   670
Geoffrey Chaucer, *from* The General Prologue to *The Canterbury Tales*   671
Geoffrey Chaucer, Merciless Beauty   672
G. K. Chesterton, The Donkey   673
John Ciardi, Most Like an Arch This Marriage   674
Samuel Taylor Coleridge, Frost at Midnight   675
Samuel Taylor Coleridge, Kubla Khan   676
Billy Collins, Care and Feeding   677
Hart Crane, My Grandmother's Love Letters   678
Hart Crane, Chaplinesque   679
Stephen Crane, I saw a man pursuing the horizon   680
Stephen Crane, A man feared that he might find an assassin   681
E. E. Cummings, All in green went my love riding   682
E. E. Cummings, O sweet spontaneous   683
E. E. Cummings, somewhere i have never travelled,gladly beyond   684
E. E. Cummings, the Cambridge ladies who live in furnished souls   685
Marisa de los Santos, Perfect Dress   686
John Donne, The Good-Morrow   687
John Donne, Batter my heart, three-personed God   688

Copyright © 2013 by Pearson Education, Inc.

John Donne, Death be not proud   689
John Donne, The Flea   690
John Donne, A Valediction: Forbidding Mourning   691
Rita Dove, Daystar   692
John Dryden, To the Memory of Mr. Oldham   693
Paul Lawrence Dunbar, Sympathy   694
Paul Lawrence Dunbar, The Poet   695
T. S. Eliot, Hysteria   696
T. S. Eliot, La Figlia Che Piange   697
T. S. Eliot, Preludes   698
Rhina Espaillat, Agua   699
Rhina Espaillat, Bra   700
Anne Finch, Countess of Winchilsea, Adam Posed   701
Robert Frost, Mowing   702
Robert Frost, Birches   703
Robert Frost, Mending Wall   704
Robert Frost, Stopping by Woods on a Snowy Evening   705
Allen Ginsberg, A Supermarket in California   706
Dana Gioia, California Hills in August   707
Thomas Gray, Elegy Written in a Country Churchyard   708
Thomas Hardy, "I Look into My Glass"   709
Thomas Hardy, The Convergence of the Twain   710
Thomas Hardy, The Darkling Thrush   711
Thomas Hardy, Hap   712
H.D., Oread   713
H.D., Sea Rose   714
Seamus Heaney, Digging   715
Anthony Hecht, The Vow   716
George Herbert, The Collar   717
George Herbert, The Pulley   718
George Herbert, Love   719
Robert Herrick, Delight and Disorder   720
Robert Herrick, To the Virgins, to Make Much of Time   721
Tony Hoagland, Beauty   722
Gerard Manley Hopkins, No Worst, There Is None   723
Gerard Manley Hopkins, Spring and Fall   724
Gerard Manley Hopkins, The Windhover   725
A. E. Housman, Into My Heart an Air that Kills   726
A. E. Housman, Epitaph on an Army of Mercenaries   727
A. E. Housman, Loveliest of trees, the cherry now   728

Copyright © 2013 by Pearson Education, Inc.

A. E. Housman, To an Athlete Dying Young   729
Randall Jarrell, The Death of the Ball Turret Gunner   730
Robinson Jeffers, Rock and Hawk   731
Ha Jin, Missed Time   732
Ben Jonson, On My First Son   733
Donald Justice, On the Death of Friends in Childhood   734
John Keats, Ode on a Grecian Urn   735
John Keats, When I have fears that I may cease to be   736
John Keats, To Autumn   737
John Keats, Ode on Melancholy   738
John Keats, On First Looking into Chapman's Homer   739
X. J. Kennedy, In a Prominent Bar in Secaucus One Day   740
Suji Kwock Kim, Monologue for an Onion   741
Ted Kooser, Abandoned Farmhouse   742
D. H. Lawrence, Piano   743
Denise Levertov, O Taste and See   744
Shirley Geok-lin Lim, Learning to Love America   745
Henry Wadsworth Longfellow, The Tide Rises, the Tide Falls   746
Henry Wadsworth Longfellow, Proem to Evangeline   747
Robert Lowell, Skunk Hour   748
Christopher Marlowe, The Passionate Shepherd to His Love   749
Andrew Marvell, To His Coy Mistress   750
Andrew Marvell, The Definition of Love   751
Andrew Marvell, The Garden   752
Edna St. Vincent Millay, Passer Mortuus Est   753
Edna St. Vincent Millay, First Fig   754
Edna St. Vincent Millay, Time Does Not Bring Relief   755
Edna St. Vincent Millay, Recuerdo   756
John Milton, On Shakespeare   757
John Milton, Lycidas   758
John Milton, When I consider how my light is spent   759
Marianne Moore, The Fish   760
Marianne Moore, To a Steam Roller   761
Marianne Moore, Poetry   762
Marilyn Nelson, A Strange Beautiful Woman   763
Howard Nemerov, The War in the Air   764
Lorine Niedecker, Sorrow Moves in Wide Waves   765
Yone Noguchi, A Selection of Hokku   766
Sharon Olds, The One Girl at the Boys' Party   767
Wilfred Owen, Futility   768

Copyright © 2013 by Pearson Education, Inc.

Wilfred Owen, Anthem for Doomed Youth   769
Sylvia Plath, Daddy   770
Edgar Allan Poe, The Raven   771
Edgar Allan Poe, "Alone"   772
Edgar Allan Poe, A Dream within a Dream   773
Alexander Pope, *from* An Essay on Man (Epistle II)   774
Alexander Pope, A little Learning is a dang'rous Thing   775
Ezra Pound, The Garden   776
Ezra Pound, Portrait d'une Femme   777
Ezra Pound, The River-Merchant's Wife: A Letter   778
Dudley Randall, A Different Image   779
John Crowe Ransom, Piazza Piece   780
Adrienne Rich, Living in Sin   781
Edwin Arlington Robinson, Mr. Flood's Party   782
Edwin Arlington Robinson, Miniver Cheevy   783
Christina Rossetti, Song   784
Christina Rossetti, Amor Mundi   785
William Shakespeare, When daisies pied and violets blue   786
William Shakespeare, When icicles hang by the wall   787
William Shakespeare, When my love swears that she is made of truth   788
William Shakespeare, Poor soul, the center of my sinful earth   789
William Shakespeare, When, in disgrace with Fortune and men's eyes   790
William Shakespeare, That time of year thou mayst in me behold   791
William Shakespeare, When to the sessions of sweet silent thought   792
William Shakespeare, My mistress' eyes are nothing like the sun   793
Percy Bysshe Shelley, Ode to the West Wind   794
Percy Bysshe Shelley, To—   795
Charles Simic, The Butcher Shop   796
Christopher Smart, For I will consider my Cat Jeoffry   797
Cathy Song, Stamp Collecting   798
William Stafford, The Farm on the Great Plains   799
Gertrude Stein, Susie Asado   800
Wallace Stevens, The Emperor of Ice-Cream   801
Wallace Stevens, Peter Quince at the Clavier   802
Jonathan Swift, A Description of the Morning   803
Alfred, Lord Tennyson, *from* In Memoriam A. H. H.   804
Alfred, Lord Tennyson, Now Sleeps the Crimson Petal   805
Alfred, Lord Tennyson, Ulysses   806
Diane Thiel, Memento Mori in Middle School   807
Dylan Thomas, Fern Hill   808

Copyright © 2013 by Pearson Education, Inc.

John Updike, Ex-Basketball Player   809
Derek Walcott, Sea Grapes   810
Margaret Walker, For Malcolm X   811
Edmund Waller, Go, Lovely Rose   812
Phillis Wheatley, On Being Brought from Africa to America   813
Walt Whitman, Out of the Cradle Endlessly Rocking   814
Walt Whitman, When I Heard the Learn'd Astronomer   815
Walt Whitman, A Noiseless Patient Spider   816
Walt Whitman, *from* Song of the Open Road   817
Walt Whitman, I Hear America Singing   818
Richard Wilbur, The Writer   819
William Carlos Williams, To Waken an Old Lady   820
William Carlos Williams, The Young Housewife   821
William Carlos Williams, Danse Russe   822
William Carlos Williams, Spring and All   823
William Carlos Williams, Queen-Anne's-Lace   824
William Carlos Williams, The Widow's Lament in Springtime   825
William Wordsworth, Lines   826
William Wordsworth, She Dwelt Among the Untrodden Ways   827
William Wordsworth, I Wandered Lonely as a Cloud   828
William Wordsworth, Ode   829
William Wordsworth, Composed upon Westminster Bridge   830
James Wright, Autumn Begins in Martins Ferry, Ohio   831
Mary Sidney Wroth, In this strange labyrinth   832
Sir Thomas Wyatt, They flee from me that sometime did me sekë   833
William Butler Yeats, No Second Troy   834
William Butler Yeats, An Irish Airman Foresees His Death   835
William Butler Yeats, Crazy Jane Talks with the Bishop   836
William Butler Yeats, The Magi   837
William Butler Yeats, When You Are Old   838

# ▶ DRAMA

Talking with *David Ives*

## 34 Reading a Play 841

THEATRICAL CONVENTIONS   842
ELEMENTS OF A PLAY   843
    Susan Glaspell, *Trifles*   844
ANALYZING *TRIFLES*   845

WRITING EFFECTIVELY
>Susan Glaspell on Writing, Creating *Trifles*   846
>>THINKING ABOUT A PLAY   847

## 35   Modes of Drama Tragedy and Comedy   848

TRAGEDY   849
>Christopher Marlowe, Scene from *Doctor Faustus* (Act 2, Scene 1)   850

COMEDY   851
>David Ives, *Sure Thing*   852

WRITING EFFECTIVELY
>David Ives on Writing, On the One-Act Play   853
>>THINKING ABOUT COMEDY   854

## 36   Critical Casebook Sophocles   855

THE THEATER OF SOPHOCLES   856
THE CIVIC ROLE OF GREEK DRAMA   857
ARISTOTLE'S CONCEPT OF TRAGEDY   858

**SOPHOCLES   859**
THE ORIGINS OF *OEDIPUS THE KING*   859
>Sophocles, *Oedipus the King*
>>(Translated by Dudley Fitts and Robert Fitzgerald)   860

THE BACKGROUND OF *ANTIGONÊ*   871
>Sophocles, *Antigonê*
>>(Translated by Dudley Fitts and Robert Fitzgerald)   872

CRITICS ON SOPHOCLES   885
>Aristotle, Defining Tragedy   885
>Sigmund Freud, The Destiny of Oedipus   886
>E. R. Dodds, On Misunderstanding Oedipus   887
>A. E. Haigh, The Irony of Sophocles   888
>David Wiles, The Chorus as Democrat   889
>Patricia M. Lines, What Is Antigonê's Tragic Flaw?   890

WRITING EFFECTIVELY
>Robert Fitzgerald on Writing, Translating Sophocles into English   891
>>THINKING ABOUT GREEK TRAGEDY   892

## 37   Critical Casebook Shakespeare   894

THE THEATER OF SHAKESPEARE   895

**WILLIAM SHAKESPEARE   896**
A NOTE ON *OTHELLO*   896

PICTURING *OTHELLO* 897
    William Shakespeare, *Othello, the Moor of Venice* 898
THE BACKGROUND OF *HAMLET* 913
PICTURING *HAMLET* 914
    William Shakespeare, *Hamlet, Prince of Denmark* 915
THE BACKGROUND OF *A MIDSUMMER NIGHT'S DREAM* 935
PICTURING *A MIDSUMMER NIGHT'S DREAM* 936
    William Shakespeare, *A Midsummer Night's Dream* 937
    William Shakespeare, *Macbeth* 946
    William Shakespeare, *Romeo and Juliet* 974
    William Shakespeare, *The Tempest* 1000
CRITICS ON SHAKESPEARE 1010
    Anthony Burgess, An Asian Culture Looks at Shakespeare 1010
    W. H. Auden, Iago as a Triumphant Villain 1011
    Maud Bodkin, Lucifer in Shakespeare's *Othello* 1012
    Virginia Mason Vaughan, Black and White in *Othello* 1013
A PORTFOLIO OF PLAYERS: FAMOUS OTHELLOS IN PERFORMANCE 1014
    A. C. Bradley, Hamlet's Melancholy 1015
    Rebecca West, Hamlet and Ophelia 1016
    Jan Kott, Producing Hamlet 1017
    Johann von Goethe, Hamlet as a Hero Unfit for His Destiny 1018
    Edgar Allan Poe, Hamlet as a Fictional Character 1019
    Clare Asquith, Shakespeare's Language as a Hidden Political Code 1020
    Germaine Greer, Shakespeare's "Honest Mirth" 1021
    Linda Bamber, Female Power in *A Midsummer Night's Dream* 1022
WRITING EFFECTIVELY
    Ben Jonson on Writing, On His Friend and Rival William Shakespeare 1023
        UNDERSTANDING SHAKESPEARE 1024

## 38 The Modern Theater 1025

REALISM 1025
NATURALISM 1026
SYMBOLISM AND EXPRESSIONISM 1027
AMERICAN MODERNISM 1028
    Henrik Ibsen, *A Doll's House* (Translated by R. Farquharson Sharp, revised by Viktoria Michelsen) 1029
    Henrik Ibsen on Writing, Correspondence on the Final Scene of *A Doll's House* 1032
    Eugene O'Neill, *The Hairy Ape* 1033

Tennessee Williams, *The Glass Menagerie* 1041
Tennessee Williams on Writing, How to Stage *The Glass Menagerie* 1048
TRAGICOMEDY AND THE ABSURD 1049
RETURN TO REALISM 1050
EXPERIMENTAL DRAMA 1051
Milcha Sanchez-Scott, *The Cuban Swimmer* 1052
Milcha Sanchez-Scott on Writing, Writing *The Cuban Swimmer* 1059
DOCUMENTARY DRAMA 1060
Anna Deavere Smith, Scenes from *Twilight: Los Angeles, 1992* 1061
Anna Deavere Smith on Writing, A Call to the Community 1064
WRITING EFFECTIVELY
THINKING ABOUT DRAMATIC REALISM 1065

## 39 Evaluating a Play 1066

WRITING EFFECTIVELY
JUDGING A PLAY 1067

## 40 Plays for Further Reading 1068

David Henry Hwang, *The Sound of a Voice* 1069

David Henry Hwang on Writing, Multicultural Theater 1078

Edward Bok Lee, *El Santo Americano* 1079

Jane Martin, *Beauty* 1080

Arthur Miller, *Death of a Salesman* 1081

Arthur Miller on Writing, Tragedy and the Common Man 1086

J. M. Synge, *Riders to the Sea* 1087

August Wilson, *Fences* 1088

August Wilson on Writing, A Look into Black America 1098

# ▶ WRITING

## 41 Writing About Literature 1100

READ ACTIVELY 1101
Robert Frost, Nothing Gold Can Stay 1101
PLAN YOUR ESSAY 1102
PREWRITING: DISCOVER YOUR IDEAS 1103
Sample Student Prewriting Exercises 1103
DEVELOP A LITERARY ARGUMENT 1109

Copyright © 2013 by Pearson Education, Inc.

WRITE A ROUGH DRAFT   1110
    Sample Student Paper, Rough Draft   1110
REVISE YOUR DRAFT   1111
FINAL ADVICE ON REWRITING   1112
DOCUMENT SOURCES TO AVOID PLAGIARISM   1113
THE FORM OF YOUR FINISHED PAPER   1114
SPELL-CHECK AND GRAMMAR-CHECK PROGRAMS   1115
    Anonymous (after a poem by Jerrold H. Zar), A Little Poem Regarding Computer Spell Checkers   1115

## 42 Writing About a Story   1116

READ ACTIVELY   1117
THINK ABOUT THE STORY   1118
PREWRITING: DISCOVER YOUR IDEAS   1119
    Sample Student Prewriting Exercises   1119
WRITE A ROUGH DRAFT   1124
REVISE YOUR DRAFT   1125
WHAT'S YOUR PURPOSE? COMMON APPROACHES TO WRITING ABOUT FICTION   1126
    Explication   1127
    Analysis   1128
    The Card Report   1129
    Comparison and Contrast   1130
    Response Paper   1131

## 43 Writing About a Poem   1132

READ ACTIVELY   1133
    Robert Frost, Design   1133
THINK ABOUT THE POEM   1134
PREWRITING: DISCOVER YOUR IDEAS   1135
    Sample Student Prewriting Exercises   1135
WRITE A ROUGH DRAFT   1136
REVISE YOUR DRAFT   1137
COMMON APPROACHES TO WRITING ABOUT POETRY   1138
    Explication   1138
    A Critic's Explication of Frost's "Design"   1139
    Analysis   1140
    Comparison and Contrast   1141
    Abbie Huston Evans, Wing-Spread   1141
HOW TO QUOTE A POEM   1142

## 44 Writing About a Play    1143

READ CRITICALLY    1144
COMMON APPROACHES TO WRITING ABOUT DRAMA    1145
    Explication    1145
    Analysis    1145
    Comparison and Contrast    1145
    Card Report    1146
    A Drama Review    1147
HOW TO QUOTE A PLAY    1148

## 45 Writing a Research Paper    1149

BROWSE THE RESEARCH    1150
CHOOSE A TOPIC    1151
BEGIN YOUR RESEARCH    1152
    Print Resources    1152
    Online Databases    1153
    Reliable Web Sources    1154
    Visual Images    1155
EVALUATE YOUR SOURCES    1156
    Print Resources    1156
    Web Resources    1157
ORGANIZE YOUR RESEARCH    1158
REFINE YOUR THESIS    1159
ORGANIZE YOUR PAPER    1160
WRITE AND REVISE    1161
MAINTAIN ACADEMIC INTEGRITY    1162
ACKNOWLEDGE ALL SOURCES    1163
    Using Quotations    1164
    Citing Ideas    1165
DOCUMENT SOURCES USING MLA STYLE    1166
    List of Sources    1166
    Parenthetical References    1166
    Works-Cited List    1167
    Citing Print Sources in MLA Style    1168
    Citing Web Sources in MLA Style    1169
    Sample List of Works Cited    1170
ENDNOTES AND FOOTNOTES    1171
SAMPLE STUDENT RESEARCH PAPER    1172
    Sample Student Research Paper, Kafka's Greatness (See Chapter 8)

CONCLUDING THOUGHTS   1172

REFERENCE GUIDE FOR MLA CITATIONS   1173

# 46 Writing as Discovery Keeping a Journal   1177
THE REWARDS OF KEEPING A JOURNAL   1178
SAMPLE JOURNAL ENTRY   1179
   Sample Student Journal   1179

# 47 Writing an Essay Exam   1180
PRACTICE ESSAY EXAM   1181
   Toni Cade Bambara, The Lesson   1182

# 48 Critical Approaches to Literature   1183
FORMALIST CRITICISM   1184
   Cleanth Brooks, The Formalist Critic   1185
   Michael Clark, Light and Darkness in "Sonny's Blues"   1186
   Robert Langbaum, On Robert Browning's "My Last Duchess"   1187
BIOGRAPHICAL CRITICISM   1188
   Brett C. Millier, On Elizabeth Bishop's "One Art"   1189
   Emily Toth, The Source for Alcée Laballière in "The Storm"   1190
HISTORICAL CRITICISM   1191
   Hugh Kenner, Imagism   1192
   Seamus Deane, Joyce's Vision of Dublin   1193
PSYCHOLOGICAL CRITICISM   1194
   Sigmund Freud, The Nature of Dreams   1195
   Gretchen Schulz and R. J. R. Rockwood, Fairy Tale Motifs in "Where Are You Going, Where Have You Been?"   1196
   Harold Bloom, Poetic Influence   1197
MYTHOLOGICAL CRITICISM   1198
   Carl Jung, The Collective Unconscious and Archetypes   1199
   Northrop Frye, Mythic Archetypes   1200
   Edmond Volpe, Myth in Faulkner's "Barn Burning"   1201
SOCIOLOGICAL CRITICISM   1202
   Georg Lukacs, Content Determines Form   1203
   Daniel P. Watkins, Money and Labor in "The Rocking-Horse Winner"   1204
   Alfred Kazin, Walt Whitman and Abraham Lincoln   1205

GENDER CRITICISM 1206
    Elaine Showalter, Toward a Feminist Poetics 1207
    Nina Pelikan Straus, Transformations in The Metamorphosis 1208
    Richard R. Bozorth, "Tell Me the Truth About Love" 1209
READER-RESPONSE CRITICISM 1210
    Stanley Fish, An Eskimo "A Rose for Emily" 1211
    Robert Scholes, "How Do We Make a Poem?" 1212
    Michael J. Colacurcio, The End of Young Goodman Brown 1213
DECONSTRUCTIONIST CRITICISM 1214
    Barbara Johnson, Rigorous Unreliability 1215
    Geoffrey Hartman, On Wordsworth's "A Slumber Did My Spirit Seal" 1216
CULTURAL STUDIES 1217
    Vincent B. Leitch, Poststructuralist Cultural Critique 1218
    Mark Bauerlein, What Is Cultural Studies? 1219
    Camille Paglia, A Reading of William Blake's "The Chimney Sweeper" 1220

# Tour of
# The Literature Collection: An eText

## Tables of Contents: Multiple Paths for Finding Selections

Our table of contents design makes it easy to explore the text by genre, theme, available media, or alphabetically. Simply click the organization that interests you and drill down to find the right selection for your course.

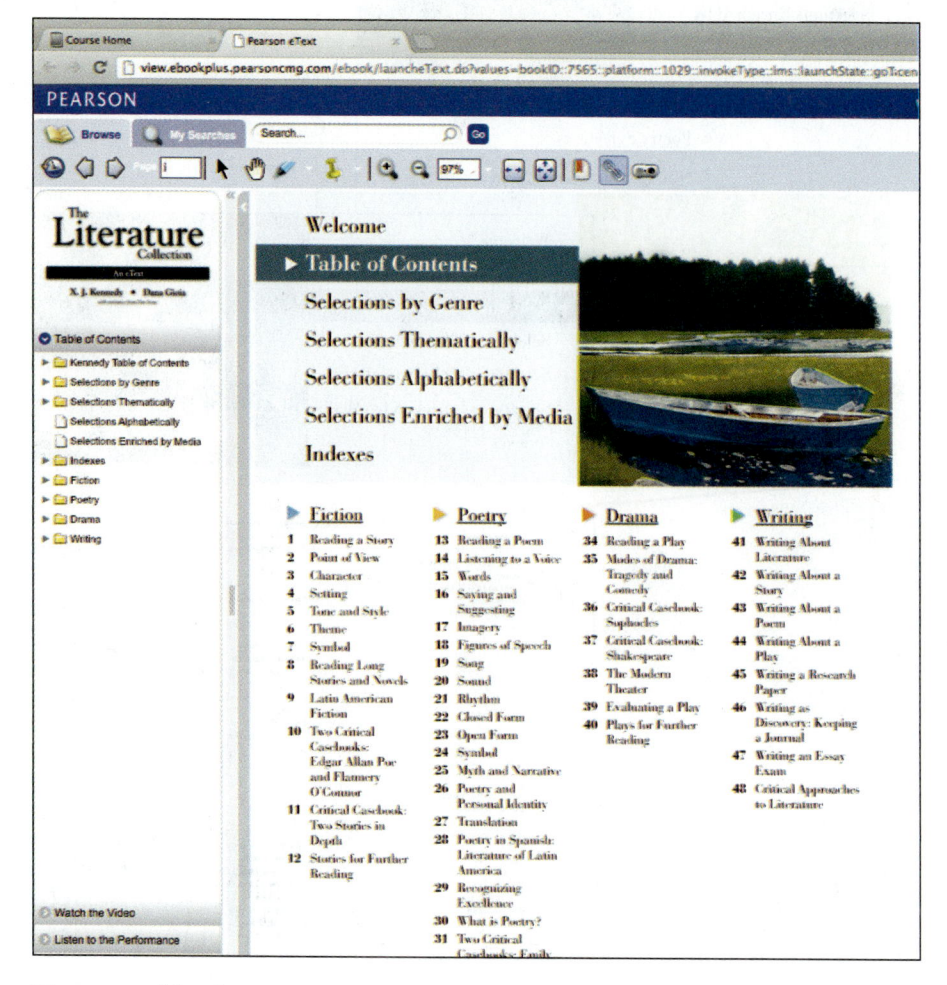

The main table of contents appears on the first page. Click on any chapter to go to its detailed table of contents. Then click on any heading to go to that page. As you move deeper into the eText, the left-hand table of contents is always available for you to use in navigating the eText.

## Selections by Genre

If you wish to view the selections available in a specific genre, click "Selections by Genre" and then choose your genre, then a selection that interests you.

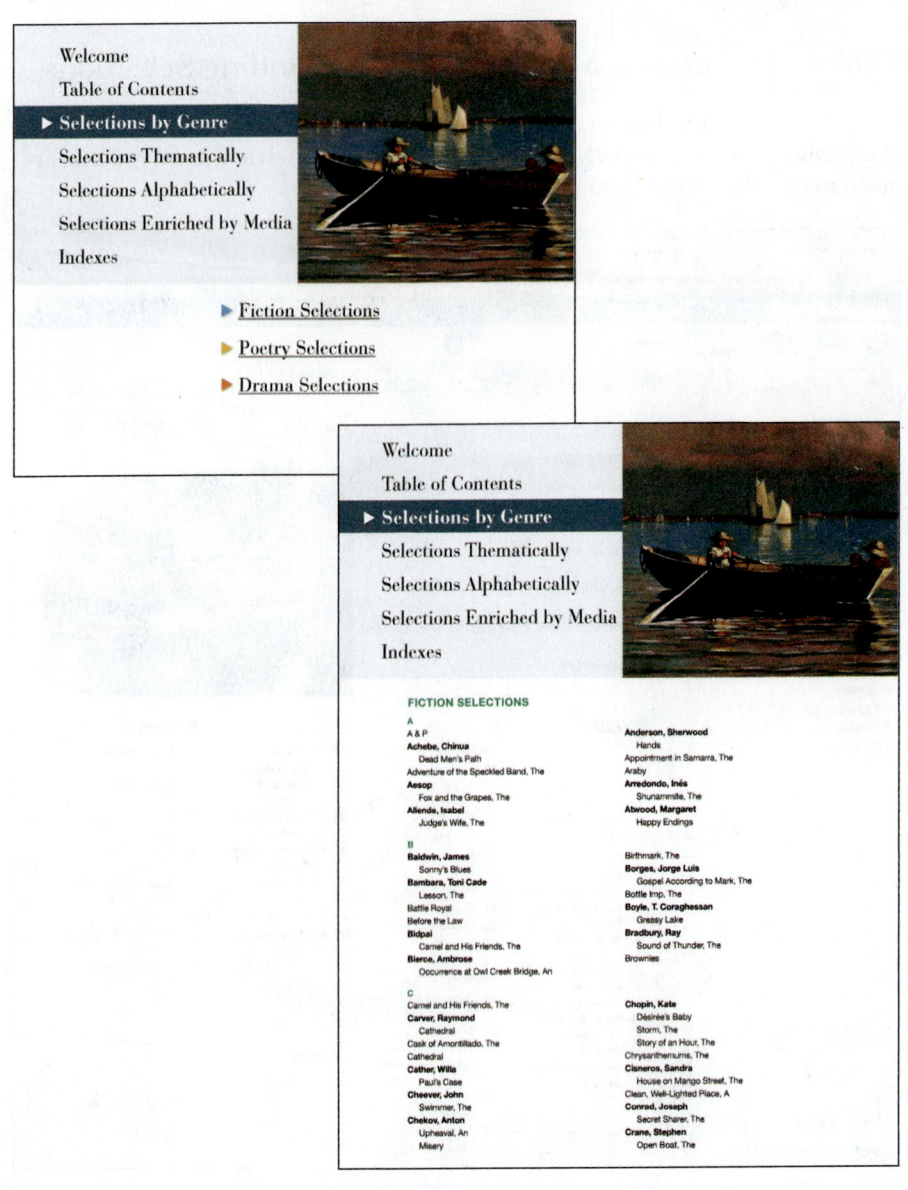

Welcome
Table of Contents
▶ Selections by Genre
Selections Thematically
Selections Alphabetically
Selections Enriched by Media
Indexes

▶ Fiction Selections
▶ Poetry Selections
▶ Drama Selections

Welcome
Table of Contents
▶ Selections by Genre
Selections Thematically
Selections Alphabetically
Selections Enriched by Media
Indexes

**FICTION SELECTIONS**

**A**
A & P
**Achebe, Chinua**
 Dead Men's Path
Adventure of the Speckled Band, The
**Aesop**
 Fox and the Grapes, The
**Allende, Isabel**
 Judge's Wife, The

**B**
**Baldwin, James**
 Sonny's Blues
**Bambara, Toni Cade**
 Lesson, The
Battle Royal
Before the Law
**Bidpai**
 Camel and His Friends, The
**Bierce, Ambrose**
 Occurrence at Owl Creek Bridge, An

**C**
Camel and His Friends, The
**Carver, Raymond**
 Cathedral
Cask of Amontillado, The
Cathedral
**Cather, Willa**
 Paul's Case
**Cheever, John**
 Swimmer, The
**Chekov, Anton**
 Upheaval, An
 Misery

**Anderson, Sherwood**
 Hands
 Appointment in Samarra, The
 Araby
**Arredondo, Inés**
 Shunammite, The
**Atwood, Margaret**
 Happy Endings

Birthmark, The
**Borges, Jorge Luis**
 Gospel According to Mark, The
 Bottle Imp, The
**Boyle, T. Coraghessan**
 Greasy Lake
**Bradbury, Ray**
 Sound of Thunder, The
 Brownies

**Chopin, Kate**
 Désirée's Baby
 Storm, The
 Story of an Hour, The
 Chrysanthemums, The
**Cisneros, Sandra**
 House on Mango Street, The
 Clean, Well-Lighted Place, A
**Conrad, Joseph**
 Secret Sharer, The
**Crane, Stephen**
 Open Boat, The

Copyright © 2013 by Pearson Education, Inc.

# Selections Thematically

You can also explore the text by theme. Select "Selections Thematically," then the theme that interests you most, then any selection.

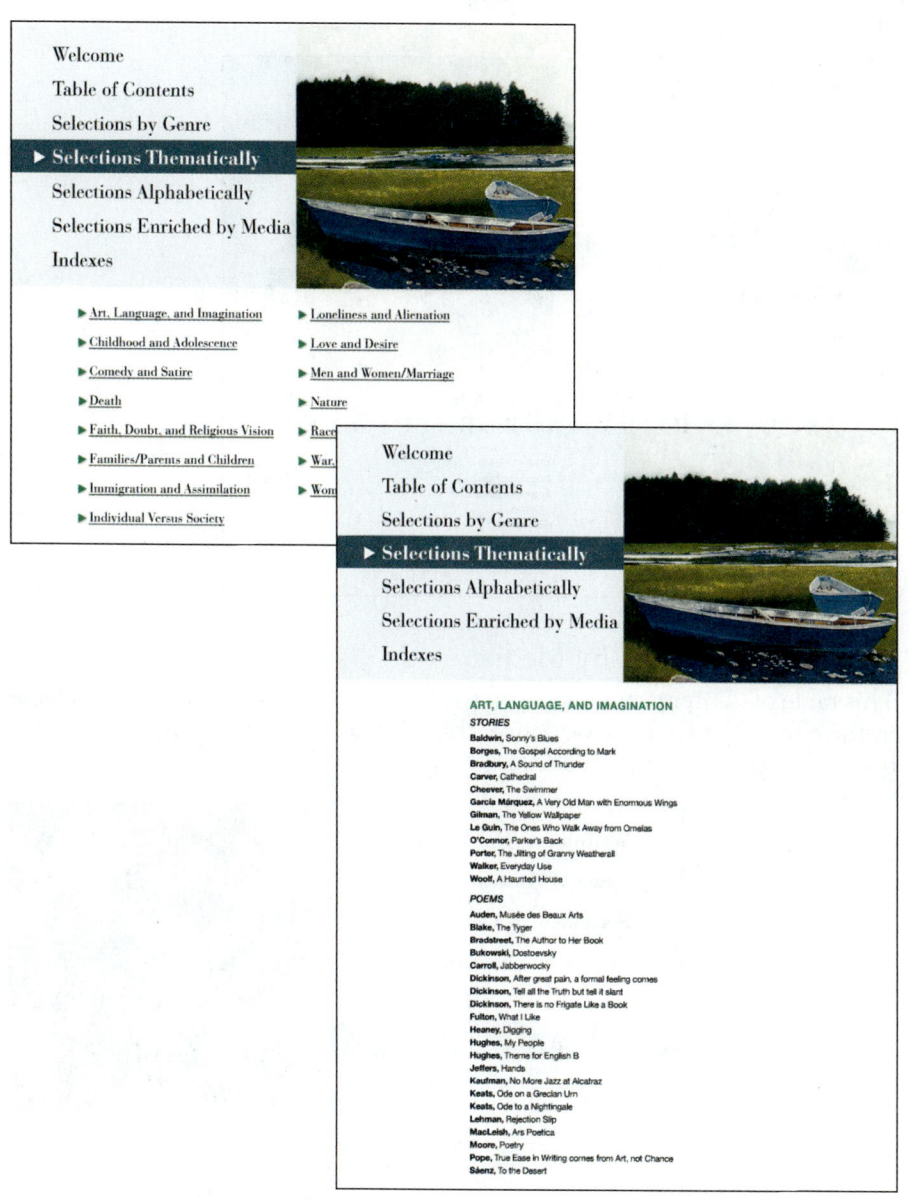

## Selections Alphabetically

"Selections Alphabetically" includes an index of every author and selection in the anthology, in alphabetical order. Click a letter to jump to that section of the alphabet.

## Selections Enriched by Media

This table of contents connects you to all audio and video resources available in the eText. For your convenience, this guide is reprinted at the back of this booklet, beginning on page 58.

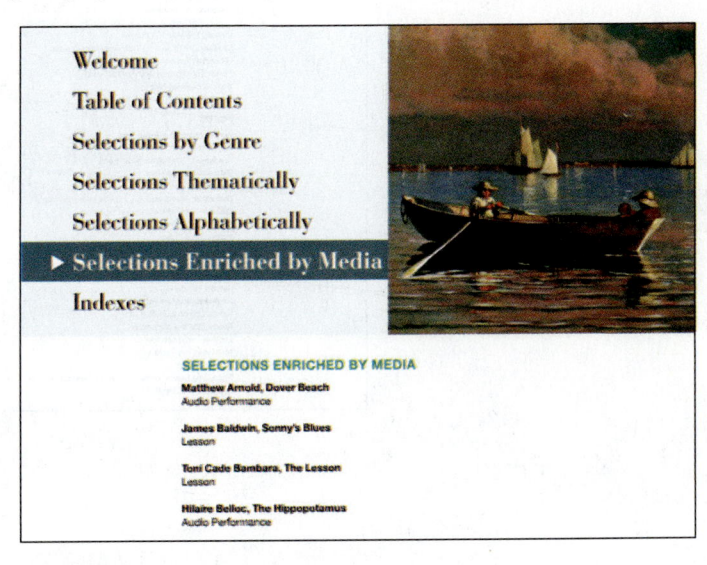

Copyright © 2013 by Pearson Education, Inc.

## Indexes

Finally, the text also offers a variety of indexes, including a General Index, an Index of First Lines of Poetry, and an Index of Literary Terms.

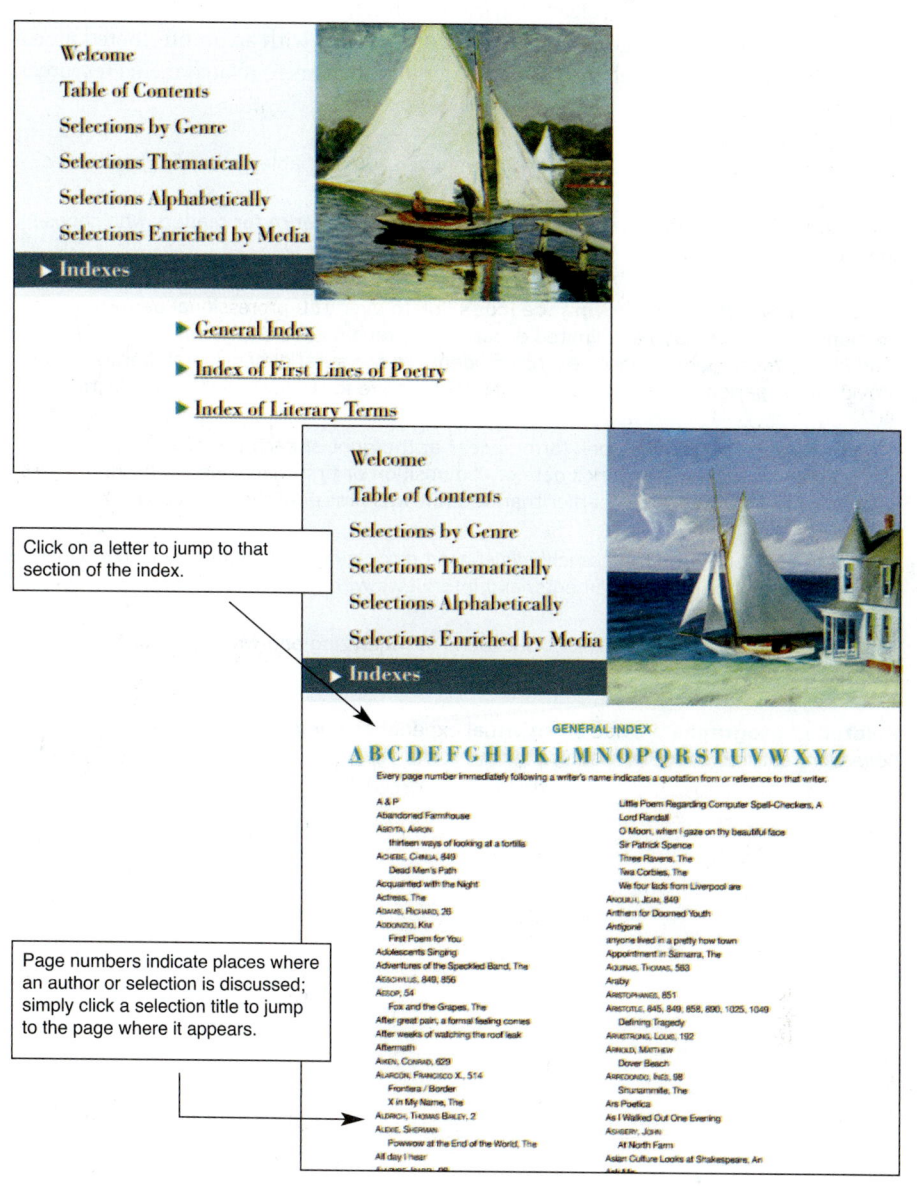

Click on a letter to jump to that section of the index.

Page numbers indicate places where an author or selection is discussed; simply click a selection title to jump to the page where it appears.

# The Multimedia Environment

The eText's design is colorful, clean, and friendly. Instruction and selections are chunked and presented on single pages in order to provide students with an uninterrupted, linear reading experience. Icons along the left margin link readers to related media resources.

**Read the Biography icons** link to one of the over 200 available author biographies.

**Footnotes** popup when clicked to provide context and guidance for readers who choose to view them.

**Listen and Watch the Performance icons** link to over 160 professional performances. So many students today have limited experience attending live theater or hearing poetry read aloud; these performances expose students to the aural dimension of literature, and provide an experience that truly brings literature to life for today's multimodal learner.

**Dates** of first publication in book form appear at the right of each title. Parentheses around a date indicate the work's date of composition or first magazine publication, given when it was composed much earlier than when it was first published in book form.

**Watch the Video icons** link to richly illustrated discussions of key literary works, video introductions to the literary elements, and interviews with key selection authors.

**Analyze the Reading icons** link to questions for analyzing and writing about the stories, poems, and plays.

**Related photographs** provide a rich visual experience. Altogether, the *Literature Collection* features over 350 visuals.

## Lewis Carroll [Charles Lutwidge Dodgson]

### JABBERWOCKY
1871

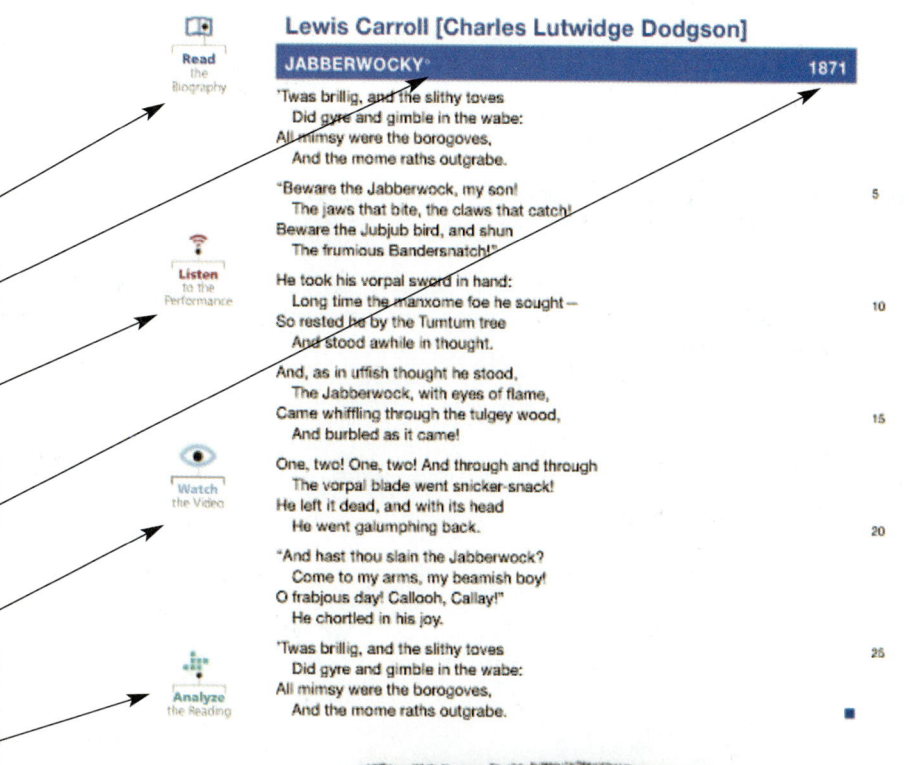

'Twas brillig, and the slithy toves
    Did gyre and gimble in the wabe:
All mimsy were the borogoves,
    And the mome raths outgrabe.

"Beware the Jabberwock, my son!
    The jaws that bite, the claws that catch!
Beware the Jubjub bird, and shun
    The frumious Bandersnatch!"

He took his vorpal sword in hand:
    Long time the manxome foe he sought—
So rested he by the Tumtum tree
    And stood awhile in thought.

And, as in uffish thought he stood,
    The Jabberwock, with eyes of flame,
Came whiffling through the tulgey wood,
    And burbled as it came!

One, two! One, two! And through and through
    The vorpal blade went snicker-snack!
He left it dead, and with its head
    He went galumphing back.

"And hast thou slain the Jabberwock?
    Come to my arms, my beamish boy!
O frabjous day! Callooh, Callay!"
    He chortled in his joy.

'Twas brillig, and the slithy toves
    Did gyre and gimble in the wabe:
All mimsy were the borogoves,
    And the mome raths outgrabe.

Jabberwocky illustration by John Tenniel, 1872

**Study the Checklist icons** link to editable checklists that allow you to adapt key summaries for your own use.

**Explore Terms for Review icons** link to simple study quizzes that go over key concepts and terms.

**View the Student Essay icons** link to student papers that illustrate the range of writing common in literature classrooms.

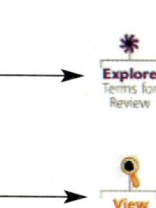

### THINKING ABOUT TONE

To understand the tone of a poem, we need to listen to the words, as we might listen to an actual conversation. The key is to hear not only *what* is being said but also *how* it is being said. Does the speaker sound noticeably surprised, angry, nostalgic, or tender? Begin with an obvious but often overlooked question: who is speaking? Don't assume that every poem is spoken by its author.

- **Look for the ways—large and small—in which the speaker reveals aspects of his or her character.** Attitudes may be revealed directly or indirectly. Often, emotions must be intuited. The details a poet chooses to convey can reveal much about a speaker's stance toward his or her subject matter.
- **Consider also how the speaker addresses the listener.** Again, listen to the sound of the poem as you would listen to the sound of someone's voice—is it shrill, or soothing, or sarcastic?
- **Look for an obvious difference between the speaker's attitude and your own honest reaction toward what is happening in the poem.** If the gap between the two responses is wide, the poem may be taken as ironic.
- **Remember that many poets strive toward understatement, writing matter-of-factly about matters of intense sorrow, horror, or joy.** In poems, as in conversation, understatement can be a powerful tool, more convincing—and often more moving—than hyperbole.

Key terms are highlighted in blue, bold font and link directly to their definitions in the Glossary of Literary Terms. The Glossary of Literary Terms provides clear and accurate definitions for 350 terms. Access these definitions on pages where the terms are used, or in the Index of Literary Terms at the front of the text.

Cross references are highlighted in maroon, bold font and link directly to the page referenced.

# The Multimedia Environment

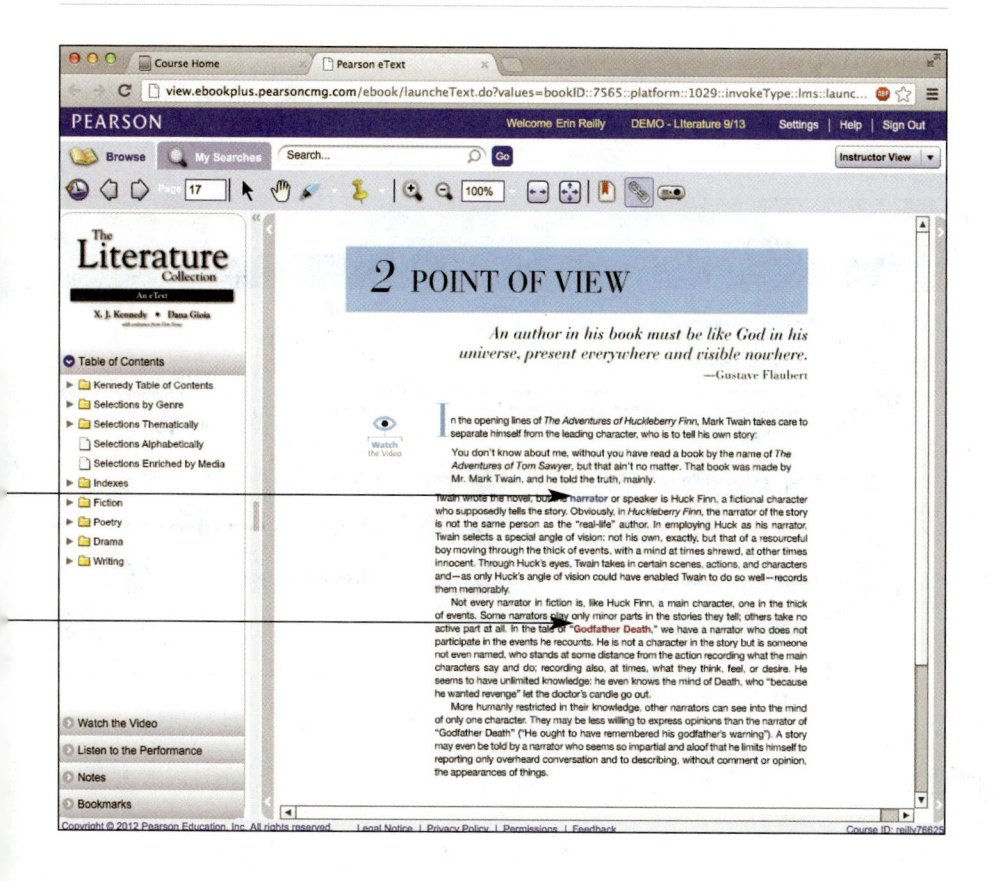

## 2 POINT OF VIEW

*An author in his book must be like God in his universe, present everywhere and visible nowhere.*
—Gustave Flaubert

In the opening lines of *The Adventures of Huckleberry Finn*, Mark Twain takes care to separate himself from the leading character, who is to tell his own story:

> You don't know about me, without you have read a book by the name of *The Adventures of Tom Sawyer*, but that ain't no matter. That book was made by Mr. Mark Twain, and he told the truth, mainly.

Twain wrote the novel, but the **narrator** or speaker is Huck Finn, a fictional character who supposedly tells the story. Obviously, in *Huckleberry Finn*, the narrator of the story is not the same person as the "real-life" author. In employing Huck as his narrator, Twain selects a special angle of vision: not his own, exactly, but that of a resourceful boy moving through the thick of events, with a mind at times shrewd, at other times innocent. Through Huck's eyes, Twain takes in certain scenes, actions, and characters and—as only Huck's angle of vision could have enabled Twain to do so well—records them memorably.

Not every narrator in fiction is, like Huck Finn, a main character, one in the thick of events. Some narrators play only minor parts in the stories they tell; others take no active part at all. In the tale of "Godfather Death," we have a narrator who does not participate in the events he recounts. He is not a character in the story but is someone not even named, who stands at some distance from the action recording what the main characters say and do; recording also, at times, what they think, feel, or desire. He seems to have unlimited knowledge: he even knows the mind of Death, who "because he wanted revenge" let the doctor's candle go out.

More humanly restricted in their knowledge, other narrators can see into the mind of only one character. They may be less willing to express opinions than the narrator of "Godfather Death" ("He ought to have remembered his godfather's warning"). A story may even be told by a narrator who seems so impartial and aloof that he limits himself to reporting only overheard conversation and to describing, without comment or opinion, the appearances of things.

## ClassPrep

In the instructor's view of the eText, ClassPrep icons link you to Instructor's Manual and Test Bank entries for key selections.

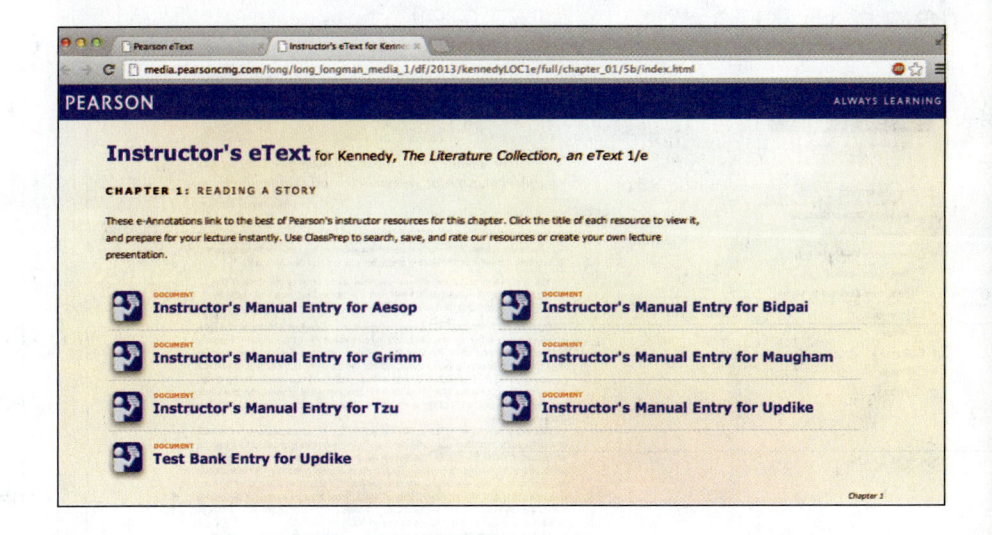

# The eText Toolbar

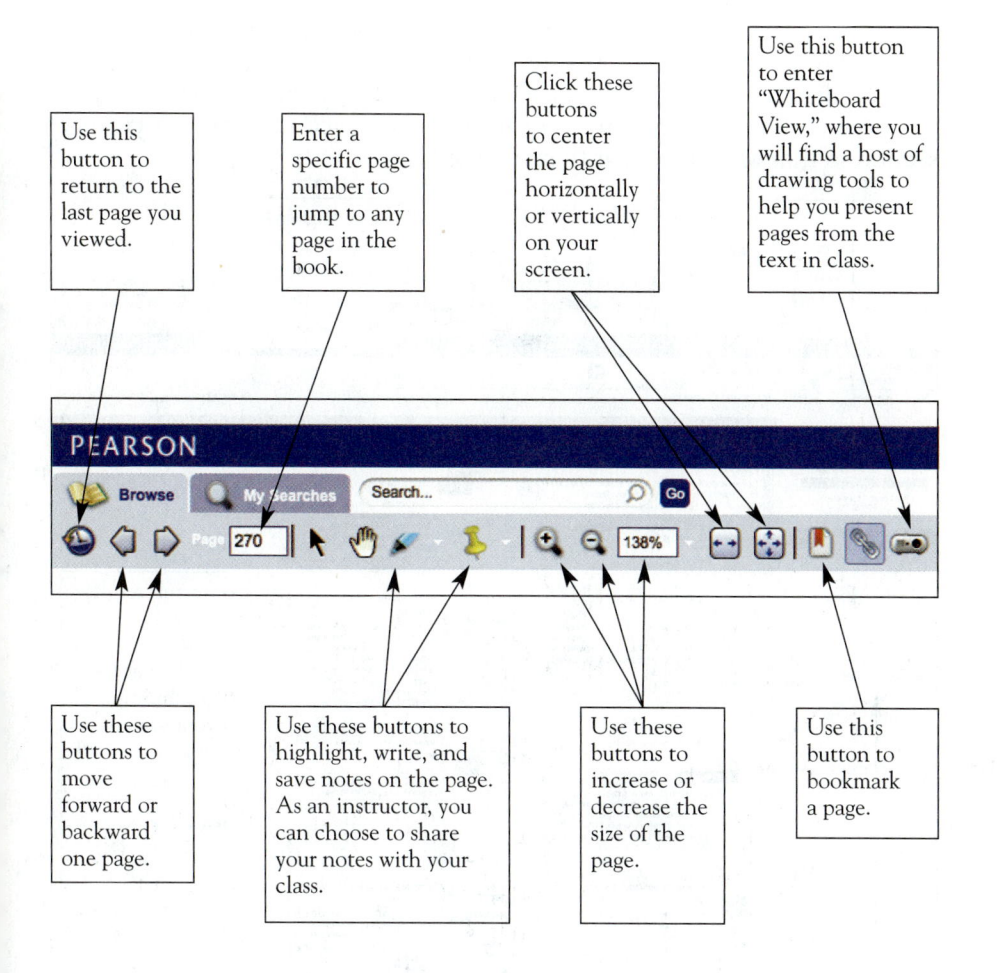

Use this button to return to the last page you viewed.

Enter a specific page number to jump to any page in the book.

Click these buttons to center the page horizontally or vertically on your screen.

Use this button to enter "Whiteboard View," where you will find a host of drawing tools to help you present pages from the text in class.

Use these buttons to move forward or backward one page.

Use these buttons to highlight, write, and save notes on the page. As an instructor, you can choose to share your notes with your class.

Use these buttons to increase or decrease the size of the page.

Use this button to bookmark a page.

# Search

*The Literature Collection* is fully searchable. Enter your keywords into the search field and your search will return any instances of that phrase in the entire text. Your results include a preview of each page to help you quickly find the reference you are looking for. Also, your searches are saved in a "Search History" section so that you can revisit them with ease.

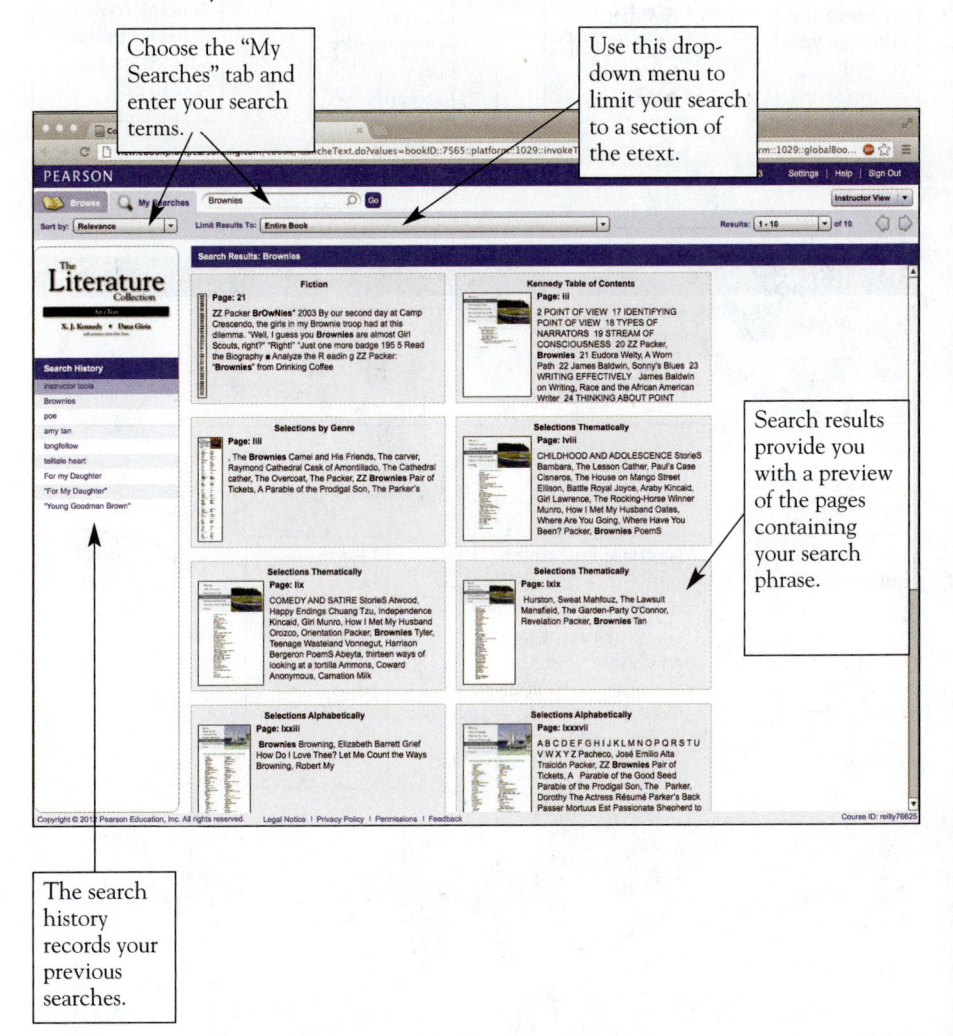

Choose the "My Searches" tab and enter your search terms.

Use this drop-down menu to limit your search to a section of the etext.

Search results provide you with a preview of the pages containing your search phrase.

The search history records your previous searches.

Copyright © 2013 by Pearson Education, Inc.

# MyLiteratureLab

## Access to MyLiteratureLab.com

*The Literature Collection* is housed within *MyLiteratureLab*, a state-of-the-art, web-based, interactive learning resource for use in literature courses. It provides a wealth of resources geared to meet the diverse teaching and learning needs of today's instructors and students.

You can use *The Literature Collection* as a discreet text, much the same way that you would use a traditional print text. Or you can use *The Literature Collection* as a management system to completely administer a course online.

## Using MyLiteratureLab as a Course Management System

Every selection and media resource has been included in the Resources section so that you can easily assign readings at a simple click. Go to Instructor Tools, then Resources. The materials are arranged alphabetically by author. Simply hover over a resource to assign, hide, or comment on it. Your changes feed directly into your students' study plans. Students can access the "To Do" list (the Study Plan and list of assignments) right on their home page. They also have a calendar that provides an at-a-glance look at due dates for assignments and required topics.

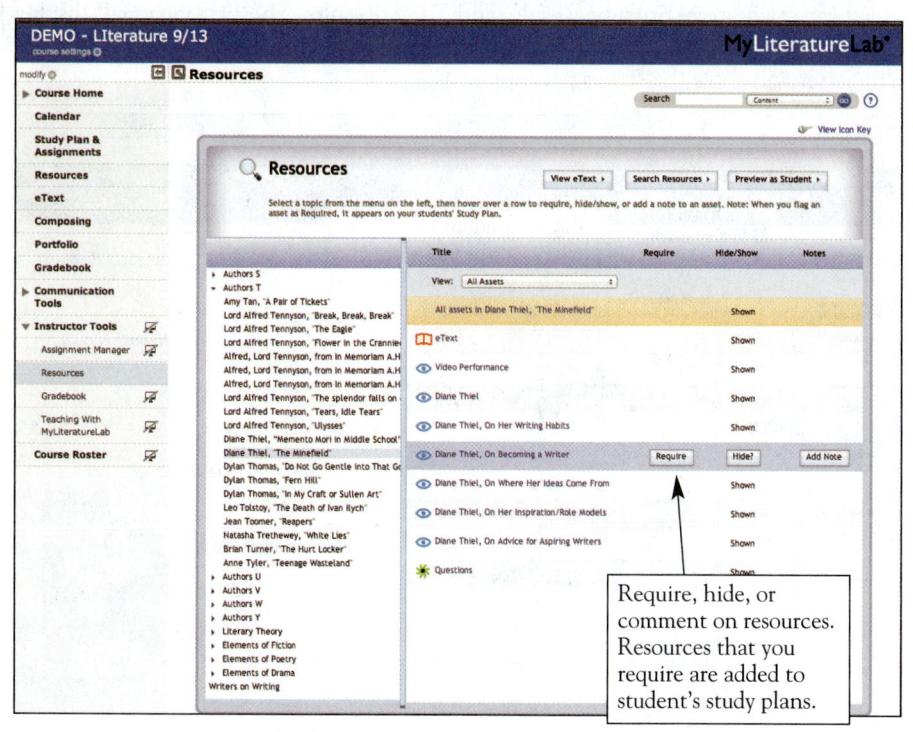

Copyright © 2013 by Pearson Education, Inc.

52  Tour of *The Literature Collection: An eText*

By assigning tasks and due dates in MyLiteratureLab, you can create a syllabus and then track your student's progress.

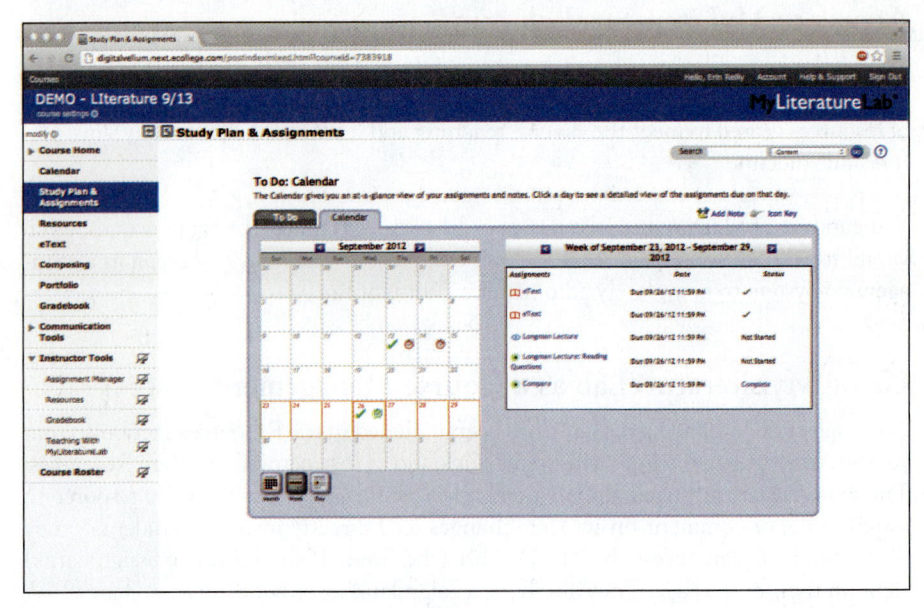

Student's assessment results are sent directly to your gradebook. The Gradebook is divided into two areas: Student Results and Topic Results. The first view will display students' grades for assignments and resources (tutorials and exercises) you required. The latter will show the scores per topic.

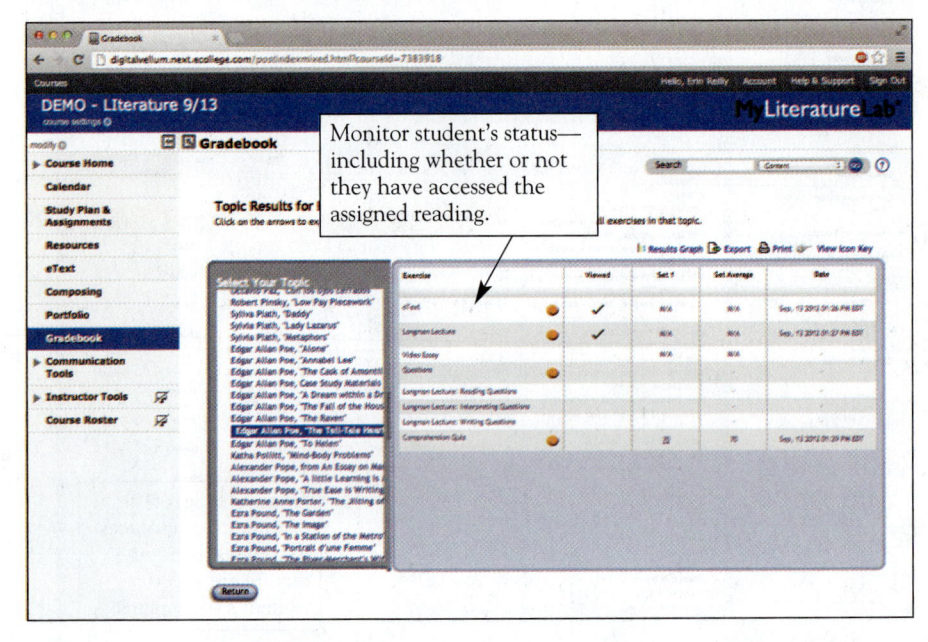

Monitor student's status—including whether or not they have accessed the assigned reading.

Copyright © 2013 by Pearson Education, Inc.

## Communication Tools

Using MyLiteratureLab's "Communication Tools" you can also share documents, send and receive email, facilitate discussion boards, and engage in synchronous chat and whiteboard sessions.

## Writing, Grammar, and Research Coverage

The *Resource* section also includes instruction, multimedia tutorials and exercises for a wide variety of composition topics. Topics are organized under the broad categories of Writing, Grammar, and Research.

- **Writing:** Instruction in the writing process, writing about literature, and the effective use of sources, as well as a library of sample papers.
- **Grammar:** Students can improve their grammar skills outside of classroom time through the grammar diagnostics, which produce personalized study plans that link students to multimedia instruction in a given topic and practice opportunities. Instructors and students can track progress via the Gradebook. Students' Study Plans will adapt based on their diagnostic results, assets required by the instructor, or comments made by the instructor on their writing submissions.
- **Research:** Avoiding plagiarism and evaluating sources tutorials, citation diagnostics and exercise sets, step-by-step instruction in writing a literary research paper, samples, and much more.

## Composing Space

The Composing space integrates market-leading resources for literature, writing, grammar, and research within an easy-to-use writing environment that looks and functions like most popular word processing programs. Students have these powerful learning tools at their fingertips 24/7 as they research, draft, and revise. In this dynamic application, students can receive feedback from their instructor, their peers, and a professional Pearson tutor. The intuitive commenting functionality allows instructors to insert personalized feedback or select from our pre-loaded comments on key grammar or style errors frequently made by students. It also allows instructors to create personalized student study plans by linking to topics in the Resource library from the student's own writing. If you require students to keep a portfolio of their work within MyLiteratureLab, you will access their documents in the portfolio section.

# Ordering and Assigning *The Literature Collection* for Your Course

## How do I get a *Literature Collection* account?

- Go to www.pearsonmylabs.com.
- Click **Educator** in the Register box.
- Choose your location and follow the steps.
- Pearson will send you your account information within an hour from when you submit your request. Be sure to check your spam if it does not arrive.

## How to sign in

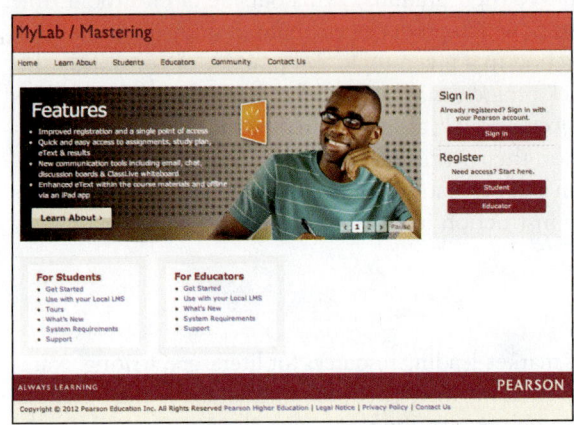

- Go to www.pearsonmylabs.com.
- In the "Sign In" box, click **Sign In**.
- Enter your username and password in the fields provided.
- Click **Sign In**.

## How to create a course

- Click Create/Copy Course on the left of your My Pearson portal page.

*Note[1]—your principal area of interest will be the left-most box.

*Note[2]—this image shows what the My Pearson Portal will look like the first time you sign in. If you have existing courses, you will see a slightly different view.

54    Copyright © 2013 by Pearson Education, Inc.

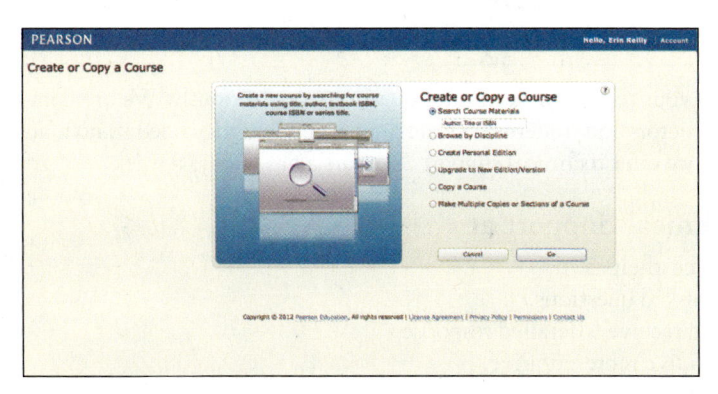

Ordering and Assigning *The Literature Collection* for Your Course    55

- In the Copy a Course box, choose Copy Another Instructor's Course and enter Course ID b18244.
- Click **Go**.

Enter the course information.
- Course Name
- Description
- Course Type
- Course Enrollment Dates
- Course Duration
- Make Available For Other Instructors to Copy
- Create Course Now

You will see a confirmation page with your personal *CourseID*. **Give this CourseID to your students.** When your course is ready, you will receive an email from *MyLab* and Mastering Support.

## How do my students get access?

You can order access code cards from your campus bookstore using ISBN 0205900348. Your students can also order access online at www.myliteraturelab.com.

## Training and Technical Support

At Pearson, we take your technical needs and questions very seriously. We are committed to giving instructors and students technical support when they need it, no matter what. Therefore, we offer technical support 24 hours a day, 7 days a week.

### Customer Technical Support at

http://247pearsoned.custhelp.com
- Search frequently asked questions.
- Ask a question and receive a detailed response.
- Chat online with a live representative.

### Live, Online Training at

http://www.MyLiteratureLab.com/training.html
- We offer weekly online training sessions for MyLiteratureLab.
- Join one of our training webinars and learn how to use the application from a member of our media team.
- Review our webinar schedule and learn more about our training options.

### Detailed How-To Videos at

http://www.MyLiteratureLab.com/howtovideos.html
- Watch videos for convenient how-to instructions for some of MyLiteratureLab's most popular tasks.
- How-to videos are available for both instructors and students.

# Other Formats

Any version of Kennedy can be packaged with *The Literature Collection* for a nominal cost. Contact your Pearson representative for ordering information.

## *Literature, 12th Edition*

*Literature: An Introduction to Fiction, Poetry, Drama, and Writing*, Twelfth Edition, provides the framework for the *Literature Collection*. The text features 65 stories, more than 400 poems, and 17 plays in its 2,192 pages. (ISBN 0321876202)

## *Compact Edition*

There is also the Seventh Compact Edition of *Literature: An Introduction to Fiction, Poetry, Drama, and Writing* in paperback, for instructors who find the full edition "too much book." Although this compact version offers a slightly abridged table of contents, it still covers the complete range of topics presented in the full edition. (ISBN 0321876210)

## *Backpack Edition*

There is an even more compact edition of this book, which we have titled *Backpack Literature*, Fourth Edition, in honor of the heavy textbook loads many students must carry from class to class. This much briefer anthology contains only the most essential selections and writing apparatus, and it is published in a smaller format to create a more travel-friendly book. (ISBN 0321886828)

## *Portable Edition*

This edition provides all the content of the comprehensive text in four lightweight paperback volumes—*Fiction*, *Poetry*, *Drama*, and *Writing*—packed in a slipcase. (ISBN 0321890213)

## *Fiction and Poetry Available Separately*

Instructors who wish to use only the fiction section or only the poetry section of this book are directed to *An Introduction to Fiction*, Eleventh Edition, and *An Introduction to Poetry*, Thirteenth Edition. Each book has writing chapters applicable to its subject, as well as the chapters "Writing a Research Paper" and "Critical Approaches to Literature."

# Media Index

This index provides a listing of all audio and video resources that are available with *The Literature Collection*.

**Matthew Arnold, Dover Beach, 646**
Audio Performance

**James Baldwin, Sonny's Blues, 23**
Lesson

**Toni Cade Bambara, The Lesson, 1182**
Lesson

**Hilaire Belloc, The Hippopotamus, 375**
Audio Performance

**Ambrose Bierce, An Occurrence at Owl Creek Bridge, 144**
Video Performance (scene)
Lesson

**Elizabeth Bishop, One Art, 568**
Lesson

**William Blake, The Chimney Sweeper, 239**
Audio Performance

**William Blake, Garden of Love, 655**
Audio Performance

**William Blake, London, 276**
Audio Performance

**William Blake, A Poison Tree, 654**
Audio Performance

**William Blake, The Sick Rose, 657**
Audio Performance

**William Blake, The Tyger, 656**
Audio Performance

**Anne Bradstreet, The Author to Her Book, 214**
Audio Performance

**Anne Bradstreet, To My Dear and Loving Husband, 658**
Audio Performance

**Robert Bridges, Triolet, 435**
Audio Performance

**Gwendolyn Brooks, The Mother, 659**
Lesson

**Elizabeth Barrett Browning, Grief, 661**
Audio Performance

**Elizabeth Barrett Browning, How Do I Love Thee? Let Me Count the Ways, 662**
Audio Performance

**Robert Browning, My Last Duchess, 206**
Audio Performance

**Robert Browning, Porphyria's Lover, 663**
Audio Performance

**Robert Browning, Soliloquy of the Spanish Cloister, 664**
Audio Performance

**Robert Burns, Oh, my love is like a red, red rose, 339**
Audio Performance
Lesson

**George Gordon, Lord Byron, When We Two Parted, 665**
Audio Performance

**George Gordon, Lord Byron, So We'll Go No More A-Roving, 668**
Audio Performance

**Lewis Carroll, Jabberwocky, 270**
Audio Performance
Lesson

**Raymond Carver, Cathedral, 31**
Lesson

**Willa Cather, Paul's Case, 146**
Video Performance (scene)

**Kate Chopin, Desiree's Baby, 150**
Lesson

**Kate Chopin, The Storm, 38**
Lesson

**Kate Chopin, The Story of an Hour, 149**
Lesson

Copyright © 2013 by Pearson Education, Inc.

**Judith Ortiz Cofer, Quinceañera, 519**
Writers on Writing Video Interview

**Samuel Taylor Coleridge, Frost at Midnight, 675**
Audio Performance

**Samuel Taylor Coleridge, Kubla Khan, 676**
Audio Performance

**Billy Collins, The Names, 266**
Lesson

**Hart Crane, My Grandmother's Love Letters, 678**
Audio Performance

**E. E. Cummings, anyone lived in a pretty how town, 265**
Audio Performance

**E. E. Cummings, Buffalo Bill 's, 442**
Audio Performance

**E. E. Cummings, somewhere i have never travelled,gladly beyond, 684**
Audio Performance

**Emily Dickinson, After great pain, a formal feeling comes, 589**
Audio Performance

**Emily Dickinson, Because I could not stop for Death, 593**
Lesson

**Emily Dickinson, I Felt a Funeral, in my Brain, 584**
Audio Performance

**Emily Dickinson, I heard a Fly buzz – when I died, 592**
Audio Performance

**Emily Dickinson, I like to see it lap the Miles, 216**
Audio Performance

**Emily Dickinson, I'm Nobody! Who are you?, 586**
Audio Performance

**Emily Dickinson, Much Madness is divinest Sense, 590**
Audio Performance

**Emily Dickinson, My Life had stood – a Loaded Gun, 318**
Audio Performance

**Emily Dickinson, Some keep the Sabbath going to Church, 588**
Audio Performance

Copyright © 2013 by Pearson Education, Inc.

**Emily Dickinson, Success is counted sweetest, 582**
Audio Performance

**Emily Dickinson, Wild Nights – Wild Nights!, 584**
Audio Performance

**John Donne, Batter my heart, three-personed God, 688**
Lesson

**John Donne, Death be not proud, 689**
Audio Performance

**John Donne, The Flea, 690**
Audio Performance

**John Donne, Song, 407**
Audio Performance

**John Donne, A Valediction: Forbidding Mourning, 691**
Audio Performance
Lesson

**Arthur Conan Doyle, The Adventures of the Speckled Band, 154**
Audio Performance

**Paul Lawrence Dunbar, Sympathy, 694**
Audio Performance

**T. S. Eliot, The Love Song of J. Alfred Prufrock, 625**
Lesson

**Robert Frost, Acquainted with the Night, 416**
Lesson

**Robert Frost, Birches, 703**
Audio Performance

**Robert Frost, Mending Wall, 704**
Audio Performance
Lesson

**Robert Frost, Mowing, 702**
Audio Performance

**Robert Frost, The Road Not Taken, 478**
Audio Performance

**Robert Frost, Stopping by Woods, 705**
Audio Performance

Copyright © 2013 by Pearson Education, Inc.

**Charlotte Perkins Gilman, The Yellow Wallpaper, 127**
Lesson

**Dana Gioia, California Hills in August, 707**
Video Performance

**Dana Gioia, Money, 329**
Video Performance

**Susan Glaspell, *Trifles*, 844**
Audio Performance
Lesson

**Robert Graves, Down, Wanton, Down!, 250**
Audio Performance

**Thomas Gray, Elegy Written in a Country Churchyard, 708**
Audio Performance

**Thomas Hardy, The Convergence of the Twain, 710**
Audio Performance

**Thomas Hardy, The Darkling Thrush, 711**
Audio Performance

**Thomas Hardy, I Look into My Glass, 709**
Audio Performance

**Thomas Hardy, Neutral Tones, 471**
Audio Performance

**Thomas Hardy, The Ruined Maid, 262**
Audio Performance

**Thomas Hardy, The Workbox, 238**
Audio Performance

**Nathaniel Hawthorne, The Birthmark, 164**
Lesson

**Nathaniel Hawthorne, Young Goodman Brown, 29**
Lesson

**Seamus Heaney, Digging, 715**
Lesson

**Robert Herrick, Upon Julia's Clothes, 720**
Audio Performance

**Gerard Manley Hopkins, God's Grandeur, 379**
Audio Performance

**Gerard Manley Hopkins, No Worst, There is None, 723**
Audio Performance

**Gerard Manley Hopkins, Pied Beauty, 297**
Audio Performance

**Gerard Manley Hopkins, Spring and Fall, 724**
Audio Performance

**Gerard Manley Hopkins, The Windhover, 725**
Audio Performance

**A. E. Housman, Eight O'Clock, 369**
Audio Performance

**A. E. Housman, Epitaph on an Army of Mercenaries, 727**
Audio Performance

**A. E. Housman, Into My Heart an Air That Kills, 726**
Audio Performance

**A. E. Housman, Loveliest of trees, the cherry now, 728**
Audio Performance

**A. E. Housman, To an Athlete Dying Young, 729**
Lesson

**A. E. Housman, When I was one-and-twenty, 394**
Audio Performance

**Langston Hughes, Theme for English B, 613**
Audio Performance

**Langston Hughes, Harlem [Dream Deferred], 615**
Audio Performance

**David Henry Hwang, *The Sound of a Voice*, 1069**
Video Biography

**Henrik Ibsen, *A Doll's House*, 1029**
Lesson

**Ben Jonson, To Celia, 343**
Audio Performance

**James Joyce, All day I hear, 370**
Audio Performance

**James Joyce, Araby, 166**
Audio Performance
Lesson

**James Joyce, Eveline, 167**
Audio Performance

**James Joyce, The Dead, 168**
Audio Performance

**John Keats, Bright star! would I were steadfast as thou art, 302**
Audio Performance
Lesson

**John Keats, La Belle Dame sans Merci, 198**
Audio Performance

**John Keats, Ode on a Grecian Urn, 735**
Audio Performance

**John Keats, Ode on Melancholy, 738**
Audio Performance

**John Keats, This living hand, now warm and capable, 402**
Audio Performance

**John Keats, To Autumn, 737**
Audio Performance

**John Keats, When I have fears that I may cease to be, 736**
Audio Performance

**X. J. Kennedy, In a Prominent Bar in Secaucus One Day, 740**
Video Performance

**Jamaica Kincaid, Girl, 172**
Lesson

**D. H. Lawrence, Piano, 743**
Audio Performance

**Emma Lazarus, The New Colossus, 575**
Audio Performance

**Henry Wadsworth Longfellow, Aftermath, 253**
Audio Performance

**Henry Wadsworth Longfellow, Proem to Evangeline, 747**
Audio Performance

**Katherine Mansfield, The Garden Party, 178**
Audio Performance

**Christopher Marlowe, The Passionate Shepherd to His Love, 749**
Audio Performance

**Andrew Marvell, To His Coy Mistress, 750**
Audio Performance

**Bobbie Ann Mason, Shiloh, 179**
Lesson

**Edna St. Vincent Millay, Recuerdo, 756**
Audio Performance

**Edna St. Vincent Millay, What lips my lips have kissed, and where, and why, 415**
Audio Performance

**Arthur Miller, *Death of a Salesman*, 1081**
Audio Performance
Video Biography
Lesson

**John Milton, Lycidas, 758**
Audio Performance

**Tim O'Brien, The Things They Carried, 184**
Lesson
Interview

**Flannery O'Connor, A Good Man Is Hard to Find, 117**
Lesson

**Joyce Carol Oates, Where Are You Going, Where Have You Been?, 183**
Lesson

**Wilfred Owen, Anthem for Doomed Youth, 769**
Audio Performance

**Wilfred Owen, Dulce et Decorum Est, 244**
Lesson

**Wilfred Owen, Futility, 768**
Audio Performance

**Dorothy Parker, Résumé, 390**
Audio Performance

**Sylvia Plath, Lady Lazarus, 510**
Lesson

**Edgar Allan Poe, Annabel Lee, 576**
Audio Performance

**Edgar Allen Poe, The Cask of Amontillado, 106**
Audio Performance

**Edgar Allan Poe, A Dream within a Dream, 773**
Audio Performance

**Edgar Allen Poe, The Fall of the House of Usher, 107**
Audio Performance

**Edgar Allen Poe, The Raven, 771**
Audio Performance

**Edgar Allen Poe, The Tell-Tale Heart, 105**
Audio Performance
Video Performance (scene)
Lesson

**Katherine Anne Porter, The Jilting of Granny Weatherall, 28**
Video Performance (scene)

**Ezra Pound, The Garden, 447**
Audio Performance

**Edwin Arlington Robinson, Richard Cory, 347**
Lesson

**Theodore Roethke, My Papa's Waltz, 211**
Lesson

**Christina Rossetti, Amor Mundi, 785**
Audio Performance

**Christina Rossetti, Song, 784**
Audio Performance

**Christina Rossetti, Uphill, 480**
Audio Performance

**William Shakespeare, *Hamlet, Prince of Denmark*, 915**
Video Performance
Lesson
Audio Performance

**William Shakespeare, Let me not to the marriage of true minds, 412**
Audio Performance

**William Shakespeare, *MacBeth*, 946**
Audio Performance

Copyright © 2013 by Pearson Education, Inc.

**William Shakespeare, *A Midsummer Night's Dream*, 937**
Audio Performance
Lesson

**William Shakespeare, My mistress' eyes are nothing like the sun, 793**
Audio Performance

**William Shakespeare, *Othello, the Moor of Venice*, 898**
Video Performance
Lesson
Audio Performance

**William Shakespeare, *Romeo and Juliet*, 974**
Audio Performance

**William Shakespeare, Shall I compare thee to a summer's day?, 316**
Audio Performance

**William Shakespeare, *The Tempest*, 1000**
Audio Performance

**William Shakespeare, That time of year though mayst in me behold, 791**
Audio Performance
Lesson

**William Shakespeare, When, in disgrace with Fortune and men's eyes, 790**
Audio Performance

**Percy Bysshe Shelley, Ode to the West Wind, 79**
Audio Performance

**Percy Bysshe Shelley, Ozymandias, 565**
Audio Performance

**Percy Bysshe Shelley, To —, 795**
Audio Performance

**Sophocles, *Antigonê*, 872**
Video Performance
Lesson

**Sophocles, *Oedipus the King*, 860**
Video Performance
Lesson

Copyright © 2013 by Pearson Education, Inc.

**Wallace Stevens, Disillusionment of Ten O'Clock, 277**
Audio Performance

**Wallace Stevens, The Emperor of Ice-Cream, 801**
Audio Performance

**Wallace Stevens, Peter Quince at the Clavier, 802**
Audio Performance

**Wallace Stevens, The Snow Man, 486**
Audio Performance

**Robert Louis Stevenson, The Bottle Imp, 186**
Audio Performance

**Alfred, Lord Tennyson, Break, Break, Break, 388**
Audio Performance

**Alfred, Lord Tennyson, from In Memoriam A. H. H. "Dark house, by which I once more steal", 804**
Audio Performance

**Alfred, Lord Tennyson, from In Memoriam A. H. H. "Be near me when my light is low.", 804**
Audio Performance

**Alfred, Lord Tennyson, The splendor falls on castle walls, 371**
Audio Performance

**Alfred, Lord Tennyson, Tears, Idle Tears, 284**
Audio Performance

**Alfred, Lord Tennyson, Ulysses, 806**
Audio Performance

**Diane Thiel, *Memento Mori* in Middle School, 807**
Video Performance

**Dylan Thomas, In My Craft or Sullen Art, 573**
Audio Performance

**Dylan Thomas, Do not go gentle into that good night, 434**
Audio Performance
Lesson

**Dylan Thomas, Fern Hill, 808**
Audio Performance

**Alice Walker, Everyday Use, 133**
Lesson

Copyright © 2013 by Pearson Education, Inc.

**Walt Whitman, O Captain! My Captain!, 571**
Audio Performance

**Walt Whitman, Out of the Cradle Endlessly Rocking, 814**
Audio Performance

**William Carlos Williams, The Young Housewife, 821**
Audio Performance

**Tennessee Williams, *The Glass Menagerie*, 1041**
Lesson

**Oscar Wilde, The Happy Prince, 188**
Audio Performance

**William Wordsworth, Composed upon Westminster Bridge, 830**
Audio Performance

**William Wordsworth, I Wandered Lonely as a Cloud, 225**
Audio Performance

**William Wordsworth, Lines, 826**
Audio Performance

**William Wordsworth, Ode: Intimations of Immortality, 829**
Audio Performance

**William Wordsworth, The world is too much with us, 493**
Audio Performance

**William Wordsworth, A Slumber Did My Spirit Seal, 366**
Audio Performance

**Sir Thomas Wyatt, They flee from me that sometime did me sekë, 833**
Audio Performance

**William Butler Yeats, An Irish Airman Foresees His Death, 835**
Audio Performance

**William Butler Yeats, The Lake Isle of Innisfree, 198**
Audio Performance
Lesson

**William Butler Yeats, Leda and the Swan, 378**
Audio Performance

**William Butler Yeats, Sailing to Byzantium, 563**
Audio Performance

Copyright © 2013 by Pearson Education, Inc.

**William Butler Yeats, The Second Coming, 500**
Audio Performance

## Elements of Literature Videos

**Character, 26**
**Closed Form, 401**
**Figures of Speech, 314**
**Imagery, 288**
**Listening to a Voice, 210**
**Open Form, 439**
**Point of View, 17**
**Reading a Poem, 194**
**Reading a Story, 3**
**Rhythm, 386**
**Saying and Suggesting, 273**
**Setting, 34**
**Song and Sound, 342**
**Symbol (Fiction), 64**
**Symbol (Poetry), 465**
**Theme, 54**
**Words, 247**

Copyright © 2013 by Pearson Education, Inc.